Knowing God Personally 2

SEEKING GOD'S PERSPECTIVE

Copyright ©2020 Godson Hez
All rights reserved. First paperback edition printed 2020 in the
United Kingdom. A catalogue record for this book
is available from the British Library.
ISBN 978-1-913455-18-7
No part of this book shall be reproduced or transmitted in
any form or by any means, electronic or mechanical, including
photocopying, recording, or by any information retrieval system
without prior written permission of the publisher.
Published by Scribblecity Publications.
Printed in Great Britain.
Although every precaution has been taken in the preparation of this
book, the publisher and author assume no responsibility for errors or
omissions. Neither is any liability assumed for damages resulting from
the use of this information contained herein.
Scripture quotations marked NLT are taken from the
Holy Bible, New Living Translation, copyright © 1996, 2004,
2015 by Tyndale House Foundation. Used by permission
of Tyndale House Publishers, Inc., Carol Stream, Illinois
60188. All rights reserved.

Dedication

Dedicated to the invisible Personality, whose presence and actions are so real and visible; to the only Teacher that understands perfectly the dividing asunder of the minds of those who sit under His tutelage; the Revealer of secrets, both of God and of men. Thank you for another help from above. It can only be you. I am humbled.

CONTENTS

Introduction	7
I Know You Not	17
Knowing His Ways	29
Knowing His Acts	38
Knowing His Plan And Purpose	55
Knowing The Good Part	64
Knowing His Suffering	75
Knowing His Dying	87
Knowing His Resurrection	96
Knowing His Presence	107
Knowing His Appearing	118
Knowing His Judgement	129

INTRODUCTION

Dear reader, it will be very pertinent to first queue you up quickly with the 'volume one' of this book 'Knowing God Personally'. I strongly recommend that you get a copy of it and read through the contents like a hungry soul. If on the other hand you have read it, but it has been long since you did that, and you seem to have recovered from the impact it left on you, I strongly suggest that you go back to it for a refreshment course. The reason is because the revelation knowledge contained in that book was meant to lead us into a lifelong, practical relationship with God. It is meant to lead us into a daily, side by side walk with Jesus. Such experiential walk will make the impact indelible, except of course, if we read through the book like a folk-tale, or story book. However, since the first publication, I keep receiving calls from Christians of various levels of faith that have gone through it sharing testimonies of immense impacts of the book in their lives.

Let me start here by reiterating what I said in that first work that the book was not my making. It was never a product of my premeditations nor plans, because I don't stand qualified to teach on a topic such as this. We were confronted by God Himself through a startling revelation that never made any sense to me until the Lord came down and gave us the interpretation of the revelation to the minutest detail. It was so real and practically impacting as He took us from the known to the unknown mysteries of the kingdom life. The book presented us with the result of a divine x-ray of our knowledge of God as individual Christians, and as the Body of Christ. The result was very indicting. We were weighed in God's balance and were found wanting in the scale of the knowledge of God who we call our Father.

Once again we heard the Lord crying out as in the days of Hosea that the present-day church is on the verge of being destroyed like the wilderness church for lack of the knowledge of God. We were able to discover from the book that God in His infinite mercies did not leave us to wallow in the guilt of that costly ignorance. He exposed us to very practicable steps that will launch us into the depths of divine knowledge. The same way we pass through some set of systematic moves from one level to another in order to acquire genuine knowledge in any field of life, we discover that we can never pick the knowledge of God up from the surface of the earth.

Our uncommitted attitude to seeking to come to the true knowledge of a God who dwells in the realm of great mysteries is the worst pandemic of mankind. The Lord gave us the antidote to wiping away this costly ignorance of knowledge of God. We can never know the Person of God until we all run into His presence and get registered into the school of The Spirit. It follows a common phenomenon. The only way to escape ignorance in any field is to go to the school of learning in that field. So, we were introduced in volume one of this book to this heaven ordained, practical revelation school in God's presence.

The Lord Jesus Christ made it emphatically clear that "No one knows the Son except the Father, and no one knows the Father except the Son and those to whom the Son chooses to reveal him" (Matt 11:27, NIV). It becomes very clear here that the genuine knowledge of God comes by personal revelation. In the revelation that gave birth to this book, the Lord made it clear that every general means through which we acquire divine knowledge can only have a pass mark for an elementary, peripheral level of His knowledge. We can never enjoy relationship with our God at that level. Please order for a copy of the book now and discover more revelations.

The later part of the book presented us with the challenging experiences of both the early church and some contemporary Christians who did exploits in the name of the Lord. It was very clear that they were all born and harvested through the authority and power of the knowledge of God that they possessed. Their respective testimonies confirmed that only those to whom God is revealed, become those in whom and through whom the strength of God is revealed. Wonderful revelation!

So, what brought about this second volume of the book? I never premeditated it, just as I did make it clear from the first volume that this work is beyond me. As I prepared to speak in one of our annual conferences on the theme: "Beyond Emotional Religion", the Lord began to reveal to me the great consequences of running our Christian lives on the general, peripheral level of the knowledge of God. The best we can become with all the mental, general knowledge of the Triune God is emotionally excited religious folks, but spiritually destitute in the inherent power of godliness.

What if we decide to continue to navigate through this world with that mental, general knowledge of God we gathered from our church leaders, parents and public opinion, how far can we go in pleasing God? What if we refuse to make any deliberate attempt to seek divine revelation of God at an intimate level, are we at any risk? Shouldn't God accept us the way we are? Shouldn't He understand? This is our usual disposition.

Think about this. Is it really possible to have a Father and not live, dine and wine daily in His bosom? It could be possible under abnormal conditions, but not without abnormal consequences. If we grow up outside that nuclear intimacy, the question is, how much would our lives become a reflection of who our Father truly is? We must therefore note at this juncture that our unwillingness either by choice or indifference

INTRODUCTION

to join our Father in the Holy of Holies for intimate communion will only bring us the greatest shock at the wake of eternity. I say this without mincing words, my brethren.

The burden was heavy as the Lord began to pour into my heart the sure consequences of rejecting pursuit of the personal, revelation of who God is. The burden to save mankind, especially Christians from the impending destruction that awaits every careless disposition to knowing God personally is what gave birth to the second volume of this book. We will be discovering here that just as every intimate relationship is consummated and perfected in the inner court, and not in any superficial, ceremonial display, our relationship with God can never be perfected outside the place of intimacy.

Look at this: "My people are being destroyed, because they don't know Me. Since you priests refuse to know me, I refuse to recognize you as my priests" (Hos.6:4, NLT). When you compare this scripture in Hosea with the picture that our Lord Jesus Christ presented of what the judgment of God will hold for some "Christians" in Matthew 7:22-23 which says, "Many will say to Me in that day, 'Lord, Lord, have we not prophesied in Your name, cast out demons in Your name, and done many wonders in Your name?' And then I will declare to them, 'I never knew you'". The following points stand out:

- The people being referred to in both scriptural texts here that do not know God are God's people, priests, prophets, gifted 'men of God', and 'well known Christians'.

- In Hosea, God said that though they are priests, they don't know Him, and made no effort to try to know him. So, it is possible to be a priest or Christian and not know the Lord. What does that signify? The lack of knowledge that was being referred to here cannot be that of total ignorance. The only possible reason is that these people took God for granted and were contented with the general, mental peripheral knowledge of God that every other person had. They cared not about any personal intimacy with God. This scenario perfectly confirms the statement of Jesus in Matthew.

INTRODUCTION

- In Matthew, we also saw that these people whom the Lord told 'I don't know you' thought they knew God. They gave their evidence, but indeed they missed it. What does that suggest? Again, the only possibility is that they possessed an inferior, general knowledge of God and cared not about God's own revelation of His Person to them. They must have operated solely on whatever they were told about God. They must have avoided the secret place where the Father meets with His children. The grace not only to know God but be known of Him is only made accessible in the place of intimacy with God.

- The prophetic statement of Jesus in Matthew was a fulfillment of the prophecy of Hosea. God said in Hosea that "Since you priests refuse to know me, I refuse to recognize you as my priests". This lack of deliberate commitment to seek the true revelation knowledge of God made them settle for something less than what the Father truly is. In other words, it is the degree of our disposition to know Him that draws the revelation from the well of His presence.

It becomes very clear from the lessons here that if we choose not to do anything about running into God's presence now, to seek to know Him one on one, we can never know Him enough to be known of Him. As we see the dismantling of the religious institutions and the cathedrals that many of us depend on for divine knowledge, we will be setting ourselves up for the greatest disappointment of our lives if we refuse to run into His presence now. That will not be our portion in Jesus name.

It was this burden that gave birth to this book. Nobody actually relates with God from afar. It is either the relationship is intimate and deep, or no relationship exists. That is the way of spirit-beings. This second volume of the book is intended to stir up the hunger that will quickly drive us into His presence. It will be exposing us to the very essence of relating with our Father on an intimate dimension. We will be discovering that there is no other way. There is no alternative route into the heart of the Father.

It is one thing to know Him, and another thing to be known of God. The latter is what matters. This is what this book is about to expose us to. When we rely on our knowledge of all the religious sacraments, doctrines and dogmas, titles and charisma, miracles and gifts as our basis for claiming to know Him, we will never be known of God. The reason is because those religious contents of God's knowledge leave no room in our hearts to seek for divine confirmation, or God's own perspective of our knowledge of Him. The contents of this book will save us from this error.

The only way we can avoid that devastating judgment, "I don't know you, depart from me", is to seek to be known of Him. We will also be learning secrets from some key Bible characters who had the testimony that they made it through and became part of the great cloud of witnesses. You too are about to tap into the wealth of His knowledge, so we can join the list of the saints that finished well.

1
I KNOW YOU NOT

Many will say to Me in that day, 'Lord, Lord, have we not prophesied in Your name, cast out demons in Your name, and done many wonders in Your name?' And then I will declare to them, 'I never knew you; depart from Me, you who practice lawlessness!" (Matthew 7:22-23 NKJV).

Here is one very terrifying prophetic pronouncement in the Bible that many of us avoid. By this I mean one of those unpopular statements in scripture regarding the future judgment of God on mankind. The scriptural text here is particularly serious because of the judgmental nature. Most of the time, the temptation is always very high to take prophetic pronouncements for granted with the passage of time. We are either tempted to think that those prophetic statements will not come to pass any more, or we tend to forget them. We often get carried away, and lose consciousness of the seriousness of those statements before the appointed time of their fulfilment.

Remember that the moment man failed, the prophecy about the birth of our Saviour (the Seed of the woman) was given by God the Father Himself in Genesis 3:15. Other prophesies on this same subject from both the Major and the Minor Prophets followed. As years turned into decades and centuries, the consciousness of this great prophesy was swallowed up. However, the length of years and the unbelief of men did not stop it from being fulfilled thousands of years after. "When the fullness of time was come, God sent forth His Son, born of a woman…" (Gal. 4:4).

The unbelief and doubting laughter of both Abraham and Sarah did not stop the prophecy of the birth of the covenant child (Isaac) from coming to pass at the appointed time. When Sodom and Gomorrah came under divine judgment, Lot and his household found so much grace in the sight of God. But when Lot's wife lost consciousness of the prophetic warning not to look back to Sodom, the grace and love received by Lot did not save his wife from turning into a pillar of salt. The list of such examples is endless.

Those of us who live on the brink of eternity should avoid the danger of allowing the passage of time lead us into the error of taking prophetic statements for granted. You will agree with me dear reader by now, that no prophetic statement of the Bible has ever gone without fulfillment. We all should be wise enough to come to terms with the fact that if any of such statements has not come to pass, it is only waiting for the appointed time; it will surely come to pass whether for good or otherwise.

The scriptural text cited in this introductory chapter is one of those pronouncements that no heaven-conscious Christian could wish away; more so, since that the statement was made by our Lord Jesus Christ Himself concerning the Judgment Day. Now that we know that no prophetic statement of the Bible has ever gone without fulfillment at its appointed time, think about how devastating the experience could be on "the day when God will judge the secrets of men by Jesus Christ" (Rom 2:16). Do you know that anyone that has a true witness of the spirit while here on earth and takes heed to it, will most certainly escape that embarrassing judgment? Since this fearful judgment is yet to be fulfilled, we have to do something now, and fast.

The serious question now is: "Has it ever bothered you that somebody who has been known as a Christian by relations, friends and all acquaintances will be told by the Lord Jesus Christ himself, 'Depart, I never knew you?" Has it ever crossed your thoughts that people who are known and respected now as prophets, bishops, Right Rev. Doctors, and so on, will be told by the Lord and Saviour Himself, 'Depart, I never knew you?' It is also more worrisome to observe that not just one, two or few persons will be receiving this regrettable judgment. The Bible said, 'many'. You agree with me that the Bible does not exaggerate words. Have you thought about this? Do you know, or do you believe that it will surely come to pass, whether we are bothered about it or not?

Ah! But this is really amazing. Can it be possible? How can a man who has been known to have followed Jesus all his life here receive this kind of judgment? How Can Jesus not know a man that is well known to the public to be a Christian? Is it possible that a man who received so much commendation for service on his day of burial, with all the testimonies from the Bishop and church members could be told by the Lord Jesus Christ at the gate of heaven, 'Depart, I do not know you'?

What could be the problem? Running our Christian lives on one sided knowledge is the cause. Building our Christian lives on the general, peripheral, mental, partial, public opinion knowledge of God is the problem. Illustrating the danger in joining others to serve God without seeking a personal revelation knowledge of Him, the Lord Jesus said, "The kingdom of heaven is like a certain king who arranged a marriage for his son, and sent out his servants to call those who were invited to the wedding; and they were not willing to come" (Matt.22:2-4, NKJV). The king therefore extended the invitation to 'whosoever will'. They responded in their numbers. "But when the king came in to see the guests, He saw a man there who did not have on a wedding garment. So he said to him, 'Friend, how did you come in here without a wedding garment?' And he was speechless. Then the king said to the servants, 'Bind him hand and foot, take him away, and cast him into outer darkness; there will be weeping and gnashing of teeth.' "For many are called, but few are chosen." (Matt.22:11-14, NKJV).

This is serious. We cannot afford to hide within the religious crowd. It becomes very clear that though the kingdom call is to the whole world, when we answer the call, we must individually work out our salvation until we are known of Him. This can only be done in the place of intimacy alone with God. Let Him know you enough to choose you out from the many that have been called.

In a further illustration of the seriousness of knowing God personally and singling oneself out of the many, He gave us the parable of the ten virgins. What made the five of them wise and the other five foolish according to the Scriptures? "The five who were foolish didn't take enough olive oil for their lamps, but the other five were wise enough to take along extra oil" (Matt.25:3,4, NLT).

The oil is a symbol of the anointing of the Holy Spirit. We don't get that extra oil of the Holy Spirit from the street of our ceremonial, religious gatherings. The Holy Spirit is a Teacher and freely anoints those who set apart time to wait in God's presence for His Teaching and filling ministry. The extra oil is for those who still wait in the upper room seeking for His daily, divine revelations. Those who run their Christian lives careless about God's own perspective of who we truly are will not finish well. The inner witness of the Holy Spirit which we receive daily only in God's presence provides the extra anointing that keeps us going when all around us has given way.

Look at how these virgins ended up: "At midnight they were roused by the shout, 'Look, the Bridegroom is coming! Come out and meet Him!' "All the bridesmaids got up and prepared their lamps. Then the five foolish ones asked the others, 'Please give us some of your oil because our lamps are going out.' "But the others replied, 'We don't have enough for all of us. Go to a shop and buy some for yourselves.' "But while they were gone to buy oil, the Bridegroom came. Then those who were ready went in with him to the marriage feast, and the door was locked. Later, when the other five bridesmaids returned, they stood outside, calling, 'Lord! Lord! Open the door for us!' "But he called back, 'Believe me, I don't know you!' (Matt.25:6-12, NLT).

Consider those words of the wise virgins to the foolish: 'We don't have enough for all of us'. There is an extent to which the general, religious, crowd anointing will carry us. A time comes when all will sleep and slumber just as it came to pass with these ten virgins. A time comes when the just will begin to live by His (personal) faith. The five foolish virgins who always depended on "Who do men say that I am", but were devoid of the personal, revelation of God, will never know when the game is up. They quickly left to look for oil at that midnight hour, because their Christian lives revolved around public opinion. They still thought they were making it, not knowing the time. They came back to discover that the gate has been shut against them, yet their frivolity never allowed them to understand what has happened to them. General religious knowledge has taught them the mercy, love, and generosity of God, but they knew nothing about His severity. They 'knew God', but not enough to know that God knew them not. They met with the greatest disappointment of life. "Believe me, I don't know you", Jesus said. We cannot afford to end this way.

Watch the reactions of the crowd who were there, physically present, and listened to Jesus as He delivered this teaching, "And it came to pass, when Jesus had ended these sayings, the people were astonished at his doctrine: For he taught them as one having authority, and not as the scribes" (Matthew 7:28-29). The crowd were amazed; they stood in stunned silence as they wondered, 'Can this be true'? They marveled at the seriousness of the message. They were more than dazed by the overwhelming authority with which the sermon was delivered. "This is very unlike the comforting sermons of our scribes", they wondered. The shock couldn't allow them wish away this statement as they opened their mouth in great amazement.

Can I sincerely talk to you my dear reader? I am sure you know very well that the shock on the faces of those listeners that stood before Jesus can never be compared with the shock which men will receive on the very Day of Judgment. I mean the day when that statement of judgment will be handed down to men on their day of reckoning. That will not be your portion in Jesus name. But have you ever thought about it; that some men will still receive that negative, prophetic statement.

Has it ever bothered you that nobody can raise any appeal to that judgment? Not because the Lord has lost every sense of human rights; not because the Lord wants to use His authority and power to intimidate us. No! We cannot appeal because it will be so obvious to us that He truly does not know us. The shock will be so devastating, because it will dawn on you that He truly does not know you. This will make the shock a very painful one. You can't compare it with anything.

As disappointing and overwhelming as it sounds, the bitter truth is that many have received this judgment already. So many are dying today who will receive the same judgment; many will still die later and receive it. I trust God that the grace that has brought this book your way will help exonerate you from being a victim of this judgment in Jesus name. Amen!

Is there nothing we can do to escape this kind of unpleasant, regrettable judgment from the Lord? We are not left helpless by the Lord. As long as we are still alive, it still remains a prophetic warning which we can avoid by taking heed to the escape route as revealed by God. The time to deliver ourselves is now. As I spent days inquiring in the Father's presence, He made me know that the secret escape route is also found in the same statement, 'I never knew you'.

"He made known his ways unto Moses, His acts unto the children of Israel". (Psalm 103:7 KJV). There are levels of knowledge. He testified of Abraham, "…I know him…" (Gen.18:19). He called David a man after His own heart (1 Sam. 13:14); of Job God boldly challenged Satan, "Have you considered My servant Job, that there is none like him on the earth, a blameless and upright man, one who fears God and shuns evil?" (Job 1:8). Paul the Apostle affirmed before his death, "I have fought the good fight, I have finished the race, I have kept the faith." (2 Tim.4:7). Those are a few examples showing that it is possible to know the Lord, and be known of Him while we are yet here. It will be a costly mistake to leave this to chance.

The knowledge of the Holy One is deeper than any man can comprehend. Yet, He never left us wondering and groping in the dark. We have a cloud of witnesses to attest to this. We can know the Lord and be known of Him. We can only know him to the extent that He makes Himself known. He cannot reveal Himself to any man beyond the level his personal disposition is willing to accommodate. God does not impose Himself on any man. The choice is ours as to where to stop knowing more of Him, or rather, where to stop Him from revealing more of Himself to us. Come with me into the place of real intimacy with Jesus. Save yourself from that eternal, irredeemable embarrassment, 'Depart, I never knew you'.

2
KNOWING HIS WAYS

"Show me your ways, O Lord; teach me your paths"
(Psalm 25:4)

The above text reveals one of the reasons David accessed the heart of God. Look at that desperate heart cry. The expression, 'O Lord' shows that the statement goes beyond normal, verbal words. As you go through the pages of the book of Psalms, you will discover this passionate cry and desire to know the ways of God over and over. It became David's path of life. Look at Him as He reflects in one of the poems of the sons of Korah in chapter 42:1,2 (AMP): "As the hart pants and longs for the water brooks, so I pant and long for you, O God. My inner self thirsts for God. When shall I come and behold the face of God?"

You can be sure that such a passionate, heart cry cannot be ignored by God. The testimony that God gave about David, a 'man after God's own heart', was before he was made a King over Israel.. How did he earn such an incredible admiration from God? The man David got lost in the heart of God while he prayed and sought daily to know His ways. The passion to Know God's ways and paths took David beyond the general knowledge of the 'God of Israel'.

David discovered that knowing God's acts is not the same thing as knowing His ways. He caught this significant revelation from the dealings of God with Moses and the children of Israel, and declared, "He (God) made known his ways unto Moses, His acts unto the children of Israel" (Psalm 103:7 KJV). The difference that these divine dealings made in their respective lives was very clear. While the children of Israel only beheld the glory of God from afar through the movement of the pillar of cloud, Moses knew his way into the cloud of glory. While the rest of the children of Israel waited at the foot of the mountain of God's presence, Moses knew his way into God's presence. You can hear them telling Moses to go and hear from God on their behalf (Exod.19:8). Little wonder they didn't go far. The difference is always clear.

Pastor Aaron was the mouthpiece of Moses during his encounter with Pharaoh. So, he enjoyed the display of heavenly acts both in Egypt and in the wilderness but couldn't learn the way that Moses walked with God. It was not surprising he spent his spare time gossiping about Moses with his sister Miriam, rather than seeking and getting acquainted with the ways of God with Moses. The little time that Moses was out of sight, and handed over temporarily to Pastor Aaron, he quickly molded the Egyptian god which he was familiar with, and pointed to the children of Israel, "…these are your gods, O Israel, which brought you up out of the land of Egypt" (Exod.32:4). What a disappointment? What happened to Aaron? How could he have degenerated so fast? He knew the acts of the God of Israel, but not His ways and paths.

Think about this? Here was the same Aaron who stood with Moses before Pharaoh, and spoke to him severally with lamentable voice while the plagues lasted, "Let my people go…" The same Pastor Aaron that sang with all

Israel at the parting of the Red sea, "... who is like unto thee, O Lord, glorious in holiness, ...doing wonders, ...the Lord shall reign forever and ever..." (Exod.15:1-18), and so many other great worship songs. What went wrong? The people enjoyed God's acts, not knowing His ways. God's acts are wonderful, but we must seek to know His ways in order not to be disappointed at last.

As David sought passionately to know the way of the Lord, he discovered this wide gap between the way Moses related with God and the way the children of Israel related with Him. They were all born and trained under the same Egyptian captivity. As a matter of fact, being trained by Pharaoh himself, Moses ought to have been influenced more by the Egyptian religion and culture than the rest of the children of Israel. Yet, he was not. One thing must be very obvious here; you must agree with me that the mother of Moses must have done a great job teaching Moses the ways of the God of Israel while she weaned him for Pharaoh's daughter.

When Moses ran away from Egypt and became a shepherd at forty, it was another time of real training having been separated from his relations. The loneliness, hunger, and desperation in the wilderness of Midian brought him into another level of training on the ways and dealings of God. Remember he was given a princely training in the house of Pharaoh from a very young age. Running away from Egypt and the house of Pharaoh to become a fugitive and a servant in Midian was a serious descent from the pinnacle of power and glory to a 'nobody' position. So, the humiliation which was brought about by this sudden experience exposed him to another side of the ways of God.

Moses continued his life as a shepherd, until God called him to fulfil the divine purpose of delivering the children of Israel from the hand of Pharaoh. Remember that David was a shepherd boy too. It is possible that among the other experiences of Moses, the wilderness school of shepherding must have drawn his interest the most. He finally discovered that God made His ways known unto Moses, but the children of Israel only knew His acts. Who determines what we know? As a New Testament believer, you will agree with me that we only know Him to the extent we are open, hungry, and thirsty for Him. "Blessed are those who hunger and thirst for righteousness, for they will be filled" (Matt.5:6).

So, what difference does it make knowing the ways of God beyond His acts? This is the only way to be double sure that God Himself knows us even as we claim to know Him. Moses was one man among a few others that God testified openly of, about how much He (God) knew him. God practically defended Moses both in his lifetime and in death. He developed such an intimate relationship with God such that while he was still battling for victory over the flesh like every other Christian today, God came down and defended the character of Moses even when people gathered against him with false accusations.

When Moses didn't know what was going on behind him, God arose in his defense like a man would arise in defense of his virtuous wife anywhere: "My servant Moses is not so, he is faithful in all mine house. With him will I speak mouth to mouth, even apparently (clearly), and not in dark speeches; and the similitude (form) of the Lord shall he behold: wherefore then were you not afraid to speak against my servant Moses?" (Num.12:7,8). What a testimony!

It did not stop there. God also defended the name of Moses in death. When Moses died, God quickly dispatched Michael the archangel to withstand and resist the devil who came contending over the body of Moses. The devil thought he could take advantage of Moses, apparently because of the way Moses died. God rebuked him (Jude 1:9). What was his secret? His daily, passionate heart cry was the secret. Hear him, "Now therefore, I pray thee, if I have found grace in thy sight, shew me now Thy way, that I may know Thee... I beseech thee, shew me Thy glory" (Exod.33:13,18). Moses encountered God there. God certainly revealed His glory to him.

The difference this revelation knowledge also made in the life of David was very clearly displayed. While King Saul and the rest of the Israelites army were hiding away and trembling at the empty threats of the Philistine giant, David saw an uncircumcised Philistine, and brought him down. It is a popular Bible story, so you know the rest of the story. When King David was dying, here were his last words of charge to his son Solomon: "I go the way of all the earth: be thou strong therefore, and shew thyself a man; and keep the charge of the Lord thy God, to WALK IN HIS WAYS…" (1Kings 2:2,3).

Paul the apostle also got lost in God's presence, as he sought endlessly to know His ways. Hear him, "Oh, the depth of the riches both of the wisdom and knowledge of God! How unsearchable are His judgments and His ways past finding out!" (Rom 11:33). We can never miss our way to Heaven if driven by this same passion. We can secure ourselves a place in the heart of Jesus as we seek to know Him as the way into the kingdom of God.

There is a way to every destination in life. You must be on that road to get to the end of it. Nobody suddenly finds himself at the destination of a journey he never embarked upon. Enoch decided to walk with God in a generation where almost everybody lived and died without knowing God. He walked with God and got lost in Him. The Bible testified that God took him (Gen.5:24), while men were lost in sins and all manner of wickedness.

You can secure yourself a place in the heart of Jesus, while other men are being told, 'Depart, I never knew you'. One way we can practically achieve this is by seeking your way into the Father's heart. Thousands of years after our Lord Jesus Christ walked the earth, declaring to us, "I am the Way, the Truth and the Life...", (Jn.14:6), we seem not to be contented with Him as the only way. We have devised various ways for ourselves, rather than seeking to know the Lord (the Way) very intimately. While we are now counting days to the wake of eternity, it is dangerous to still be talking like Thomas, "Lord, we do not know where you are going, so how can we know the way?" (Jn.14:5).

3
KNOWING HIS ACTS

"Are you so blind as to ...underestimate the wealth of God's kindness? Are you unmindful or ignorant of the fact that God's kindness is intended to lead you to repent, and to accept God's will? (Rom.2:4 AMP)

May God deliver us from this dangerous presumption as we can see in this scriptural text. Knowing God's acts is very wonderful, but life propelled by this emotional excitement remains shallow and has never won God's approval. Incidentally, many of us (Christians), are caught up in this web. Rather than allow the kindness and acts of God's mercies towards us lead us into repentance, we begin to justify ourselves in unrighteousness. When you hear some of us testify about the goodness of God and His miraculous visitations upon our lives, we talk as if God has done those things because of our righteousness, even when we know that our hearts are not right with God. This is a very deadly presumption.

The Lord is drawing our attention through Paul the Apostle, to know that it is spiritual blindness when we don't see through the acts of God's patience and loving kindness to discover our wickedness and unworthiness. Rather than lead us into true repentance, we underestimate and take His goodness upon our lives for granted. So many have concluded that they are born again children of God, without any trace of a definite encounter with Jesus. A lot of others who were once born again, but have backslidden are now running their Christian lives on the miracles and open doors to wealth that the Lord lavished liberally upon them at one time or the other.

A demonstration of God's acts or events can bring us into relationship with Him, but they cannot sustain the relationship. There are different types and levels of relationships, but the strongest is the blood relationship. The relationship we have with God is a blood covenant relationship. It is a Father/son/daughter relationship. It is enjoyed and consummated at the intimate level; not just by knowing and stopping at the peripheral acts.

God can use any act to usher us into the salvation experience, but we must seek our way into His heart like David. He reminded God, "… thou art the God of my salvation; therefore, on thee will I wait all the day," to do what? To "show me your ways and to teach me your paths, and to lead me in thy truth" (Psalm 25:4,5). Wow! After salvation comes the walk. We must seek to walk with God beyond the excitement of His gifts and actions that drew us to Him.

Whatever we cherish so much occupies our heart. It is very natural to feel good with all the great, miraculous manifestations of God, but that exposes us to only one aspect of the knowledge of God. Any believer in the Lord Jesus Christ who does not want to hear from Jesus on the day of judgment, 'Depart, I never knew you', must work his or her way into the heart of Jesus. We cannot achieve this by being satisfied with just going to church, hearing, or even preaching sermons.

Here is a little illustration. A simple display of an action could make people fall in love even at first sight.

However, no matter how excited we get at that first stage of any relationship, such excitement can be eroded the next day as you begin to know each other better. So, the love relationship, whether between friends or even family can only get deeper by what the parties begin to discover about each other. The more your ways of life are made open and known to one another, the more you begin to understand each other's likes and dislikes, the deeper and better the relationship becomes. This is what takes the relationship from the ordinary level of familiarity to intimacy level.

Successful marriages may be founded on facial attraction, or on the excitement of love at first sight, but must be built and sustained on intimate knowledge of each other. This is the reason the scriptures admonished that the relationship between the husband and the wife should be as the relationship between Christ and the church (Ephes. 5:25). In the book of Rev. 21:9, we also saw the Church being referred to as the Bride of Christ. God expects us to know Him deeply as a wife would know the husband. Then, we can be sure the Lord our Bridegroom would never deny us.

It is expected that the church as the Bride of Christ, should not be introducing ourselves before the Lord at the judgment seat. No Christian should be meeting with the Lord for the first time at the gate of Heaven, "… for we are his workmanship, created in Christ Jesus…" (Ephes.2:10). So, it will sound absurd for any believer who should have been the Lord's wife to be introducing himself to the Lord on the judgment day. How does it feel standing before your own husband and saying, "Lord, I am your wife John/Jane, the one who has been prophesying and doing great miracles in your name on earth? Lord, You should remember me as I always called you, Lord, Lord",. This sounds so funny, doesn't it? Incidentally, this appears to be the scenario here. If the Lord, our husband should be declaring, "I never knew you", something is seriously wrong somewhere. He ought to have known us very intimately before that great day of meeting at the judgment seat.

Brethren, life after death is eternal. It is a real precious life. You cannot afford to play gambles with eternity by the way you live your life now. It is so unfortunate that the world has not learnt so much from history. Every day, history is made. There is hardly anything happening today that has not happened before. In fact, sometimes history keeps repeating itself several times over and over. It has however been observed that men are either too slow or even very indifferent in learning the lessons of the past. Moses, David, Paul, and the rest of the apostles that made it, all had their personal encounters with God respectively.

Our reasons for this kind of behavior are simple and look so convincing, but this is a very dangerous presumption. When we become sick to the point that physicians cannot help, and suddenly the Lord intervenes with miraculous healing the tendency is there for so many to conclude that the healing came because we are born again Christians. When God grants us breakthroughs and material provisions above our contemporaries, we take it to mean that we are in good relationship with God. This kind of subtle presumption can easily seal one's doom without the victim knowing it. This was the reason for David's prayers: "Keep back Thy servant also from presumptuous sins; let them not have dominion over me: then shall I be upright, and I shall be innocent from great transgression" (Psalm 19:3). We will never seek His holiness as long as we keep thinking that

God's acts of mercy and benevolence on us are our entitlement, or compensation for our righteousness.

Did you notice that while the Lord was handing down this judgment, they were busy trying to convince the Lord that they knew Him? What were they giving as their evidence? ACTS! ACTS and ACTIONS! Hear them: 'Lord, Lord, have we not prophesied in your name? And in your name, have cast out devils? And in your name have done many wonderful works? (Matt. 7:22). And they will hear the truth from the Lord, "Depart, I never knew you". Why? You will discover that the way they gave their evidence here reveals that they thought they were the ones doing all those miracles. Isn't this a sure proof that they never knew the Lord intimately? It will be too late to discover on that great day that we have been so foolish to think that we were the ones doing all those miracles, or that we did them together with God.

How disappointed will our pastors, prophets and all the avowed miracle workers be when they discover that all these claims that they have been using to intimidate the church members into believing that they are of

God after all, will not hold water before the Lord? How disappointed men will be when they discover that all those superficial displays they have been using to intimidate our pastors and the church elders today will not mean anything before the Lord on that day? Nobody can intimidate the Lord with stories of "we did this or that in your name". What are your own evidences today that assures you that the Lord knows you just as you claim to know Him? "Lord, remember I built cathedrals single-handedly and handed over to the church; I sponsored so many crusades and supported the trips of the General Overseer all over the world", and all other stories like that.

Do you know why those wonderful acts will not have meaning to God as evidence that we are truly His children? The reason is because these miracles we claim to be doing are the acts of God. He did them all, but only decided to pass through us as channels. Didn't John the Baptist tell us that a man can receive nothing, except it be given him from heaven? (Jn.3:27). We should be expecting so many surprises on that great day, because some of these scriptures we do not give attention to will suddenly make so much meaning to us.

We tend to forget that from the beginning of life, we were confronted with a God who is a specialist in doing wonders even before the creation of man. It is His nature. He only created man and became mindful of him. God chose to use man as a vessel to rule His world. Here is the God who started with great display of wonderful activities all in a bid to ensure that everything that man would need for comfort was provided before his creation. He created man in His image, yet He discovered that the man needed another specie of his kind to complement him, for his joy to be full. God went ahead to create the woman for the man's happiness and satisfaction (Gen. 2:18,23). We can go on and on just to show us that the demonstration of God's miraculous activities has been, even before we were physically born, and while we were yet God's enemies. "...for when we were yet without strength, and very ungodly, Christ died for us" (Rom.5:6). What else can be greater?

It is the height of deception and foolishness to suddenly begin to give so much attention to the acts and creatures of God than to the Person of God. Let us take more lessons from this same David who sought diligently to know the ways of God beyond His acts. Remember, it was in this process of seeking to know God intimately that David discovered the reason for the wide gap between how Moses knew and related with God and how the rest of the children of Israel knew and related with God. While David was in the wilderness as a shepherd boy, he confronted and slew the lion and the bear that attacked his sheep and delivered them. Nobody heard of this exciting experience until it was time to bring down the glory of the One Who alone did the miracle. He didn't go about singing his own praises until he stood before Goliath.

Hear him: "Let no man's heart fail because of him; thy servant will go and fight with this Philistine." And Saul said to David, 'No! Thou art not able to go against this Philistine to fight with him: for thou art but a youth, and he a man of war from his youth.' And David said unto Saul, 'Thy servant kept his father's sheep, and there came a lion and a bear and took a lamb out of the flock: and I went out after him, and smote him, and delivered it out of his mouth: and when he arose against me, I caught him by his beard, and smote him. Thy servant slew both the lion and the bear: and this uncircumcised Philistine shall be as one of them, seeing he has defied the armies of the living God'" (1Sam.17:32-36).

What an experience! David had learnt from that singular act of God that it is no longer him that lives, but the Lord is living His life in him. David now knew he could do all things through Christ that strengthens him. Many of us will sing the testimonies of the acts of God on the streets and pulpits, but disappoint Him when we are to draw inspiration from the miracles to bring down God's glory, especially when it looks like our physical life is at stake.

I perceive something was stirring up in the heart of David saying: 'The time has come to wave the banner back to heavens in defense of the glory of God'. David quickly told Saul in the next verse; "The Lord that delivered me out of the paw of the lion, and out of the paw of the bear, He will deliver me out of the hand of this Philistine". Oh, he conquered the fears of Saul, who said, "Go, and the Lord be with you". The Lord certainly delivered him and took His glory. We must go beyond the emotional excitement that follows every act of God to learn the spiritual lessons. This grace can only be received in the place of intimacy with God.

The children of Israel remained in ignorance knowing

nothing about the God of Abraham, but very serious in their physical observance of the covenant of circumcision. They refused as it were to seek to have individual, personal encounters with God and to know Him beyond that Abrahamic encounter. John the Baptist came thousands of years after God's encounter with Abraham, warning the Jews to bear fruits that befit repentance and stop hanging on the claim that we have Abraham as our father, (Matt.3:7-9).

Paul the apostle cried out years after John the Baptist that his kinsmen (the Jews) have a zeal of God but lack intimate knowledge of God. "For they, being ignorant of God's righteousness, and going about to establish their own righteousness, have not submitted themselves unto the righteousness of God" (Rom.10:1-3). Aa! Reliance on knowing God's acts alone can keep anybody fooled until the coming of the Lord.

The deliverance of the Jewish nation from the hand of Pharaoh was with so much demonstration of the acts of God. "Ye have seen what I did unto the Egyptians, and how I bare you on eagles' wings, and brought you unto Myself" (Exod.19:4). The Lord reminded the children of Israel, the whole essence of the miraculous acts was to bring you to Myself. "If you will now obey my voice, and keep my covenant, then ye shall be a peculiar treasure unto me above all people: for all the earth is Mine. And ye shall be unto me a kingdom of priests, and a holy nation" (Exod.19:5,6).

The lesson here is straight and simple. The miraculous acts we enjoy do not qualify us as God's peculiar treasures. It does not make us part of the kingdom of God's priests, neither does it automatically enlist us into the citizenship of the holy nation. We must go beyond the excitement of the acts into the place of intimacy with God where He alone qualifies us as His kingdom citizens and priests. After the acts, comes the walk. We must come to the Father who is behind all the acts. We must seek to be with Him, know more of Him, and love Him beyond the acts.

Jesus came, they disputed with Him vehemently until they killed Him, but they defended Moses. They claimed, "...we are disciples of Moses. We know that God spoke unto Moses, as for this fellow (referring to Jesus), we know not from whence He is" (John 9:28, 29). What did they want from Jesus? They said unto Him, "What sign (miracle) will you perform, so that we may see it and believe you? What supernatural work have you to show what you can do? Our forefathers ate the manna in the wilderness; as the scripture says, He gave them bread out of heaven to eat" (Jn.6:30, 31, AMP).

Didn't Jesus give them demonstration of acts, signs and wonders? Of course, He did more than Moses. What then was the problem? What did Jesus do wrong? He took them beyond the demonstration of God's acts, to the place of definite, personal encounter. While they demanded from Jesus, "…evermore give us this bread", He was busy telling them: "Verily, verily I say unto you, Moses gave you not that bread from heaven; but my Father giveth you the true bread from heaven. The bread of God is He which cometh down from heaven, and giveth life to the world. …I AM THE BREAD OF LIFE, he that cometh to Me shall never hunger; and he that believeth on Me shall never thirst" (Jn. 6:32-35).

Oh no! They were not interested in that heavenly bread of life. They murmured seriously at this, because it never made any sense to them. "Nobody should take away the physical manna. We do not need the God behind the manna, and we don't care to know"; so speaks their disposition. As a result, many of the disciples went back at this point, and walked no more with Him (Jn. 6:41,66). Those were the same people standing and justifying themselves as Abraham's children. What a people? Has anything changed in our time? Is this not the same kind of attitude today with which many of us are standing and waiting for God's judgment, claiming to know Him based on His acts?

Ah! The excitement of the acts poses great danger. It leads nobody through the wilderness of life. Job observed during his trial that the life of every man who is born of a woman is of few days, and those few days are full of troubles (Job 14:1). Only the Father who knows the escape route to this perilous road can train us through to victory. There is manna for every wilderness. God does not hesitate to also stop the manna when it is no longer needed. Most times we do not want to stop eating the manna. Meanwhile, God knows it will cease shortly. Every manna, miracle, act, signs and wonders of God must achieve definite spiritual purpose of drawing us closer to God, or else it loses relevance.

As we live in this end time, we must heed the warning of Paul the Apostle to learn from the very ugly experience of the children of Israel in the wilderness. They did eat the same spiritual meat; they drank the same spiritual drink: for they drank of the spiritual Rock that followed them, and that Rock was Christ. But with many of them God was not pleased: for they were overthrown in the wilderness. Now, these things that happened to them were for our examples so that we will not be overthrown into the lake of fire (1Cor 10:1-6, paraphrased). Our Christian attitude today presents so much doubts as to how much we have learnt.

The greatest onslaught against the church now is the multiplicity of all manner of deceivers in the name of miracle workers. They take advantage of the economic and financial hardship posed by these perilous times to deceive many who are still looking for God in acts than the Person of God. It is a shame that over two thousand years after the death and triumphant resurrection of our Lord Jesus Christ, all we still have today is the history of Christ's death, and empty shouts of 'the blood of Jesus!' whenever we get frightened by the devil. We have refused to see through this greatest act of God's mercies and return to God in repentance for the cleansing power in the blood. The Lord said that many would be caught up in the trap again. One reason anybody would be told by the Lord, "I never knew you" is simply because that individual never went beyond the general, religious activity level. Those who would want to escape the judgmental remarks, 'I never knew you', must go beyond that level and seek to know the Lord on an intimate level.

4

KNOWING HIS PLAN AND PURPOSE

The Lord said to Abram, "Leave your land, your relatives, and your father's home. Go to the land that I will show you. I will make you…" (Gen 12:1-2, GWV)

Hearing, seeing, and understanding the plan and leading of an invisible God by mortal man has continued to pose a very serious hitch in the relationship flow between God and man. Though God is invisible, He is actively visible; He rules and reigns in the kingdom of men. Until man comes to terms with the daily visibility of an invisible God, we will never go far in our relationship with Him.

This is a natural challenge facing every human being, especially after our salvation. If we must serve God well, we must be able to overcome this natural barrier. The God with whom we have to do, is Spirit. He has always been seeking for men who will effectively worship and relate with Him in the Spirit (Jn.4:24, AMP). We must be led by the Spirit of God. Paul, the Apostle said that, "they that are led by the Spirit, they are the children of God" (Rom. 8:14). Put it clearly the other way; all our claims to be God's children are false until we begin to show clear evidence of hearing and taking heed daily to the calling and leading of God.

Brethren, salvation is what happens when we respond to God's calling to come to Him. The call has gone out to all humanity since Adam got lost in the garden. "... the Lord God called unto Adam, and said unto him, "Where are you?" (Gen.3:9). Substitute your name for "Adam", and it will have more meaning. It couldn't have been because God wasn't seeing Adam clearly where he thought he was hidden, but that call was to wake up Adam's spiritual consciousness. Unfortunately, he couldn't wake up from that spiritual, deadly slumber.

The Father in His mercy and infinite wisdom quickly made a perfect plan to rescue and restore us back to life: 'whomsoever' will answer that call. (Jn.3:16). It is expected that when we answer a call, we wait for the next direction. Paul the Apostle wrote that we are called to salvation and holy living by His grace and to fulfil His purpose which has been before the world began (2 Tim.1:9). We are not in this faith by chance. There was a purpose and plan already on ground for us to fulfil. After the calling, comes the walk. If we don't discover, walk, and live in line with the plans and purposes of our calling, we would run in vain. God forbid!

Look at this: "...for as part of God's sovereign plan we were chosen from the beginning to be His, and all things happen just as He decided long ago." God's purpose in this was that we should praise God and give glory to Him for doing these mighty things for us, who were the first to trust in Christ. And because of what Christ did, we too, who heard the Good News about how to be saved, and trusted Christ, we were marked as belonging to Christ by the Holy Spirit, who long ago had been promised to all of us Christians (Ephes,1:11-13,TLB).

The New Testament church was birthed by the Spirit. We are called to die to the flesh and live in the spirit. Else, it will be impossible to understand and key into His purpose and plans for us. Unfortunately, we Christians who now live in this New Testament dispensation of the Spirit are not doing much to overcome this natural challenge of living in the Spirit while in this earthen vessel. The flesh must be mortified to make it possible for us as humans to access God's plans and purposes every day!

Why do we need to discover God's purpose and plans as we go through the journey of life? Is it really necessary? Having graduated from schools, acquired degrees, expertise and skills in different fields of learning, are we not equipped enough to go through life without bothering ourselves about divine purpose and plans? After becoming Bishops and Professors in theology, do we still need to be making inquiries from God like children who are still growing teeth? These are very serious questions we must sincerely seek answers to.

Let us take a little case study from the life of our spiritual Father, Abraham. He is the Father of our faith, yet, started his life's journey like every one of us. He was born in sin, and worshipped idols like every other man in his generation until one day he heard the call of God and took the decision to follow that divine calling and direction. The making of Abraham's life as our great and undisputable Father of faith began the day "the Lord said to Abram, "Leave your land, your relatives, and your father's home. Go to the land that I will show you. I will make you…" (Gen 12:1-2, GWV). Consider this: "So Abram departed as the Lord had spoken to him, and Lot went with him. And Abram was seventy-five years old when he departed from Haran" (Gen.12:4, NKJV). God was going to redirect the life of a man of seventy five years; how? Today all we do is to sing and claim Abraham's blessings, but have refused to allow God to take us through the process of Abraham's making.

What can we deduce from this? The making of a man does not begin from the day of his birth. It begins from the day he hears and responds positively to the call of God his Maker. True life begins the day the man answers the call of God, and begins to take heed to the plans and purpose of God for his life. John the Baptist said we should stop claiming Abraham as our Father when we have refused to bear the fruit that befits repentance (Matt.3:8,9).

Man was created to fulfil destiny. So, the call to fulfil destiny is the most important call that every man must answer. When we miss out on discovering God's plans and purposes for our lives personally, for any reason whatsoever, either by our carelessness or by our spiritual insensitivity, we also miss God's making. When God is not the one making us, only one thing then is very obvious. The devil takes over the stage. We are on our own. Guess the implication. When we go through life without understanding the plan of God our Father, the natural tendency is that we end up in the hand of the devil, who is our Father's arch-enemy. Oh! The devil does not miss taking advantage of that loophole.

The Bible is very clear about what the result of some of our actions and inactions are, whether we take those actions consciously or not. When we create any loophole in our relationship with God, The Bible says that the devil goes about seeking for such loopholes to devour victims. When we do not pay attention to God's plans for us after answering the call to salvation, we would go through life pursuing the wind.

We cannot afford to play gambles with this one and

only life that we have. It should be very clear to us that, whatever attitude we decide to put up does not make the issue of man's eternal destiny less serious. Every man born into this world has an eternal home where we must return at the end of our temporary abode on this planet earth. In other words, this earth where we are today is a temporary home; the Bible clearly states that we don't have a continuing city here. The devil is determined to deceive and mislead every creature born on this earth.

The movement of Abraham to Canaan was only the beginning of a lifetime journey. Other training followed in line with God's plan for His life until the Heavens could testify of him, "...for now I know that thou fearest God, seeing thou hast not withheld thy son, thine only son from me" (Gen 22:12). Every truth runs parallel. It is in the place of fulfilling Heaven's plan and purpose that we will become known of God. The truth is that, if God began the making of Abraham from the day he began to follow God's leading, the making of the Christian begins the day we answer the call to follow Christ. Making is a process. It does not begin and end one day with our 'common salvation' (Jude 3).

Remember that Lot followed Abraham not understanding what divine purpose and plans meant. He ended up not only becoming a source of temptation to Abraham, he got carried away by the cares of this life. It becomes very clear here brethren, that we can never make Heaven until we are Heaven-made. The process that began by taking heed to God's calling, must be accomplished by following His leading day by day. We cannot suddenly take a journey when we never knew the route from the onset. We will definitely miss our way. We must learn and become addicted to God's leading in line with divine purpose, if we must enjoy His making.

When we locate ourselves in God's plan and purposes, we will never be confused. We will continue to draw with joy out of the well of our salvation, and never arrogate any iota of glory to ourselves. Our fellowship with God will get deeper as we are being used of God to fulfil His own plans, and not us using God to pursue and fulfil our own earthly desires and plans. When we are in God's plans and living according to divine purpose, we will escape the condemnation, "Depart, I never knew you"; "...for there is therefore now, no condemnation to those who are in Christ Jesus, who do not walk according to the flesh, but according to the Spirit" (Rom.8:1 NKJV).

No, you can't be disappointed when you walk according to the Spirit. You can be sure that God cannot leave you after His making of you. He didn't leave Abraham after calling him out from the idol-worshipping background and after making him. There is no way the Lord will be telling you 'I never knew you' after calling you and leading you in line with His purpose and plans. If you never took over control of your life from the Lord after answering the call unto salvation, you can be sure you will fulfil destiny. "We know that in all things God works for the good of those who love him, who have been called according to his purpose" (Rom 8:28, NIV). It is in the place of intimacy that lives are aligned according to divine purpose.

5

KNOWING THE GOOD PART

"... one thing is needful: and Mary hath chosen that good part, which shall not be taken away from her."
(Luke 10:41-42)

Friends, God's word is inseparable from God Himself. One way to ensure that God knows us through and through is to become acquainted with His words, both the written and spoken words. "In the beginning was the Word, and the Word was with God, and the Word was God." (Jn.1:1). If we ever gave our lives to Christ Jesus, it is God's Word that we encountered, it is God's Word that we heard, it is God's Word that we received, it is God's Word that convicted and convinced us. Our salvation experience is a total encounter with the gospel of truth, God's Word. If yours never came that way, then it is very doubtful what you are running with. You must straighten it up now, or wait for the Lord to tell you, "I never knew you".

This salvation experience that began with a definite encounter with God's word can only be sustained and consummated in God's Word. No other way. Our Lord Jesus "said to those Jews which believed on him, If ye continue in my Word, then are ye my disciples indeed; And ye shall know the truth, and the truth shall make you free" (John 8:31-32). Nothing should ever take the place of God's Word in our relationship with Him no matter how familiar we get with His 'other part'.

The encounter we see here from the introductory scriptural text, was an experience that Jesus had with two of His very close friends, namely, Mary and Martha. I purposely omitted the part of that text that contained Martha's name, because many of us are still sitting comfortably where Martha sat. So, you may as well be Martha if held by the same habit displayed by Martha here. We should sincerely examine ourselves now, and accept that polite rebuke from Jesus, if we will save ourselves from the disappointing, embarrassing judgment, "Depart, I never knew you".

One thing we can never take away from God is His openness and willingness to make known His will to 'whosoever' will come to Him. Mary and Martha were both sisters. They loved God so much and never hid that disposition. They had the opportunity to demonstrate how much they loved God when Jesus walked the earth. So, our Lord Jesus Christ visited their home. What an opportunity it was for both of them to express how much they loved him.

Martha went out quickly to receive Jesus into her house. She had a sister called Mary who was also excited to have Jesus in their home. While Martha got seriously engaged with so many activities to make sure that Jesus was given the best entertainment, Mary sat at the feet of Jesus, listening to the words of life. Martha didn't like the idea that she was doing the runs alone while her sister sat at the feet of Jesus hearing His words.

The exact words used by some Bible versions in describing the activities of Martha should be very interesting here. King James said, "Martha was cumbered about much serving" (Luke 10:40). Being cumbered suggests serving or working under stress of much load. It suggests an ungraced service and cannot be endured for long. Jesus described her service this way: "Martha, Martha, thou art careful and troubled about many things" (Luke 10:41). The Amplified version said that 'Martha was overly occupied and too busy and was distracted with much serving'.

You will agree with me that those compliments about Martha and her Christian service and attitude are very serious. Those words do not suggest the selfless, freewill, committed attitude that accompanies Christian service. In the first place she worked as if under pressure to be noticed. She made sure she was visible in a bid to receive commendation from the Lord. It was again obvious she was determined to outshine her sister Mary. It is very clear here that Martha was practically, visibly committed to pleasing the Lord in her own way. In fact, it was surprising to her that she did not seem to be getting the commendation she expected from the Lord. Little wonder she did not waste time to register her displeasure with Jesus, her August visitor in the following words, "Lord, dost thou not care that my sister hath left me to serve alone? Bid her therefore that she help me" (Luke 10:40).

Those words of Martha came from a truly troubled heart. She expressed her utter disappointment in Jesus as we can see from those serious words of rebuke. Look at Martha asking Jesus "do you not care…"; those are very indicting and rebuking words. In other words, she was telling Jesus, He does not care. She was telling Jesus, "If you do care, you should have noticed all my labour to please you". She was giving herself all the credit and preferred herself to whatever her sister was engaged in doing. She demonstrated this by talking to Jesus in that commanding speech, "give instruction to my sister to come and join me, rather than sitting at your feet and listening to you". These are very serious indicting words to Jesus.

Many general overseers and bishops of Christian ministries today would like or wish to have 'Marthas' as members in our churches. As a matter of fact, we use them as examples to others, because they appear to be working hard in the physical. However, they are always grumbling in secret, especially when they feel they are not being noticed. They are mostly found in the conspicuous service departments in the church. They don't work where they will not be noticed. You find them amongst the choir, as good entertainers. They have wonderful voices, but always use that to draw undue attention to themselves and to intimidate others. When they don't seem to be getting that attention, they become uncontrollably stubborn.

They belong to the 'Ananias and Sapphira' groups in the church. They are wonderful in answering altar calls for donations with the sole motive of being noticed. No altar call for spiritual renewal and consecration moves them, because they feel their financial donations should justify and cover up for them. Do you blame them for behaving that way? They feel justified because they are often our preachers' delights.

You also find 'Marthas' occupying the pulpits as preachers of the gospel. As preachers, they are good advertisers of Jesus, but denying the power of His holiness. They are specialists in using all manner of enticing words of human wisdom to shine as good preachers. Their sermons are cemented with choice words and phonetics, but void of the spiritual revelation that makes God's word different from other literature books. The spiritual insight that transforms the written

Word (logos) into the spoken, creative Word of God (Rhema) is often lacking in their sermons. They do not care of course, about the spiritual impact of their ministrations. They are often more interested in the applause and accolades of their praise singing fans, than the spiritual conversion of their audience. The Bible refers to those kinds of preachers as ministers unto the people, but not ministers unto God (Ezek.44:11-14). What a part of the Christian ministry to belong to! This cannot be the good part.

As subordinate pastors, they can go any length to win the good commendation of the Overseers, but care nothing about their personal relationship with God the Father. They don't understand what separation unto God means. They are always busy here and there, and make bold to use that as a very good reason for not having time to be in the presence of God. Unfortunately, their charismatic attitude and eye service often endears them to the church leaders more than the sincere, humble ones. They use all that to intimidate the overseers just like Martha tried to do to Jesus.

Like Martha, many of us in God's vineyard do not care

to know or seek heaven's approval for the spiritual work we are doing. Many of us are working very hard to get the approval and promotion of men, rather than God the Father. Such people get easily disappointed and defeated in the course of the Christian service. They easily get offended and give up when their expectations are not being met. However, they can do anything to make sure they achieve their selfish, earthly goals. In their bid to remain relevant and acceptable to men, like King Saul, many of them have switched over to the 'witches of Endor.' (1 Sam.28:7) It is easier for us to get enticed by the enemy when we are not interested in seeking and getting the Lord's approval in our Christian lives and ministry.

Consider the lives of the holy men and women that walked and worked with God in the past, you will feel the heat of their desire for the knowledge of God Himself. They lamented and cried for the knowledge of the Holy One. Paul the Apostle said, "That I may know Him, and the power of His resurrection, and the fellowship of His sufferings, being made conformable unto His death; if by any means I might attain unto the resurrection of the dead. Not as though I had already attained, either were already perfect: but I follow after, if that I may apprehend that for which also I am apprehended of Christ Jesus" (Phil 3:10-12).

Brethren, to what generation of Christians do we really belong today? I think our daily heart cry should be, "Father, we are ashamed of our lack of desire for you". We have been covering up with so much of being here and there in the name of working for God. Do we belong to the Martha camp or the Mary camp? Don't leave that question to chance if you don't expect the Master's hammer of judgment on the very last day. If the Lord says that Mary has chosen the good part, for sitting down at Jesus feet and listening to the words of the Master, it then necessarily follows that Martha, chose the bad part, the wrong part.

The place of intimacy with God is the good part of this Christian walk. It comes first before service and must remain paramount as we continue in ministry. It can never be compromised no matter the level, or how busy we get in Christian ministry. This generation must be reminded that we must do the work of God on His own terms, and not ours. Look at what He told the children of Israel, "For I desired mercy, and not sacrifice; and the knowledge of God more than burnt offerings" (Hos 6:6-7). What is the Lord saying here?

If we have not been bathed with the knowledge of the Holy One in the place of intimacy, our sermons and messages will come without mercy. We can only succeed in exciting the people's emotions without helping them spiritually. We may succeed in taking away the substance of the members of the congregation, and sending them to hell afterward. When we perform our sacrifices of giving, and administrations in the church without the knowledge of the Holy One, we end up offering the sacrifice of fools. Solomon, in his wisdom warns, "Keep thy foot when thou goest to the house of God, and be more ready to hear, than to give the sacrifice of fools: for they consider not that they do evil" (Eccl 5:1). We can never compromise the place of intimacy with God and get it right.

Did you hear that every one of our works for God will be made to pass through the fire to know of what sort it is? Every man's work will be made manifest. Some will suffer loss; some will stand the refining fire

(1 Cor.3:13,15). The case of Martha and Mary gives us a clue that the place of intimacy is where the work begins and culminates. God is waiting for us to return there and begin to learn of Him. Make a deliberate choice for this good part, and save yourself from receiving the disappointing judgment, "Depart, I never knew you". May God help us not to labour in vain as Christians. Our Lord Jesus Christ advised, "Labour not for the food which perisheth, but for that food which endureth unto everlasting life, which the Son of man shall give unto you" (John 6:27).

6
KNOWING HIS SUFFERING

That I may know him …and the fellowship of his sufferings, (Phill.3:7)

It is difficult to fathom this prayer request of Paul the Apostle, viewed from the background of the teachings of our contemporary Christianity. The prayer, not only to know Christ, but to know the fellowship of His suffering demonstrates a very passionate, personal yearning of a heart that is completely sold out to Jesus. This is an incredible prayer request. What an expression! What a desire! What a prayer! What a pursuit! This can only be born from the place of intimacy with God, not religious followership. The man must have been lost in the love of everything that Christ meant. Think about that.

This is unlike our normal, daily prayers today. When all our pulpit sermons and music ministrations today are saying, "we won't suffer; we will never beg for bread, because God of miracles is our Father". Our 'all-night' prayers and fasting today are all about binding and casting every demon that says we will not prosper. Any time you see us manifest some aggression in our prayers today, check it out; all the aggression in our prayers is about sending every mountain that suggests suffering in our lives into the seas and deserts. We quote all the wonderful promises in the Bible attached to our claims.

Most of our sermons tend to suggest that it is evil to be a Christian and be suffering. The result is that the majority of our down-trodden, suffering believers are made to live daily under so much guilt being seen and treated as faithless weakling. On the long run, many of them either backslide, or settle for whatever short cut the devil is offering them in exchange for the way of the Cross. In almost forty years of my Christian life experience, I have watched the church gradually remove some ancient landmarks from the apostolic doctrines. In my candid opinion the worst aspect of the gospel truth that has faced serious dilution and erosion is the call to become acquainted with the fellowship of Christ's suffering. Is it any wonder that we see a big difference between the Christian lives we portray today from that of the early Christian disciples?

The Bible said we have been given not only the privilege of trusting in Christ but also the privilege of suffering for Him (Phil 1:29, NLT). Entering into the fellowship of Christ's suffering is a privilege, necessary to mold us fully into the image of Christ Jesus. Our call to salvation will never be complete until we also willfully answer the call to identify and share in His suffering; "For to this you were called, because Christ also suffered for us, leaving us an example, that you should follow His steps" (1 Peter 2:21, NKJV). No suffering is palatable, but the Bible made it clear that our suffering as Christians while we pass through our pilgrim journey here is inevitable. This tactful avoidance of those aspects of the Christian faith that brings us into real practical intimacy with our Lord Jesus Christ must be the reason many will be greeted with the judgment, "I never knew you".

Recasting some of his experiences, look at this practical demonstration of Paul the Apostle being acquainted with the fellowship of Christ's suffering. "I have been put in prison more often, been whipped times without number, and faced death again and again. Five different times the Jewish leaders gave me thirty-nine lashes. Three times I was beaten with rods. Once I was stoned. Three times I was shipwrecked. Once I spent a whole night and a day adrift at sea. I have traveled on many long journeys. I have faced danger from rivers and from robbers. I have faced danger from my own people, the Jews, as well as from the Gentiles. I have faced danger in the cities, in the deserts, and on the seas. And I have faced danger from men who claim to be believers but are not. I have worked hard and long, enduring many sleepless nights. I have been hungry and thirsty and have often gone without food. I have shivered in the cold, without enough clothing to keep me warm. When I was in Damascus, the governor under King Aretas kept guards at the city gates to catch me. I had to be lowered in a basket through a window in the city wall to escape from him" (2 Cor 11:23-27,33, NLT).

It is a very dangerous assumption to think that we can make heaven without going through the way of the Cross. Only the way of the Cross leads home; no other gospel way. In very clear words, our Lord told us, "If any of you wants to be my follower, you must turn from your selfish ways, take up your cross daily, and follow me" (Luke 9:23 NLT). In emphasizing the indispensability of the cross-driven life of every child of God, the Lord Jesus re-echoed it again, "And if you do not carry your own cross and follow me, you cannot be my disciple" (Luke 14:27 NLT). It is very clear that one way through which the Lord trains His children is by putting us through some hard trials. All through the scripture is a lineup of men and women of God who became very great after passing through various degrees of suffering.

Our Father Abraham after answering the call to follow God to inherit the Promised Land did not enter the land the next day. He was trained through famine; he suffered long to receive his covenant child and suffered the pains of circumcision at age ninety nine. Joseph had a wonderful dream of God's great plans for him. He suffered betrayal and rejection under household enemies. He suffered as a slave, suffered false accusation and imprisonment in defense of the truth. He had great opportunities in the midst of the suffering offered by the enemy to 'make it' fast. He rejected them and chose the suffering way of the Cross. So many of our testimonies of 'divine breakthroughs' today were the same kind 'packaged distractions' to Joseph, but he didn't fall for any. Unfortunately, we are quicker today to grab any alternative opportunity to avoid divinely ordained plans to take us through the fellowship of His suffering.

God delivered the children of Israel with a very strong hand from Pharaoh. He afflicted the Egyptians with all manner of plagues until they were forced to let His children go. Lives of every first born of both human and animals were taken by God, just to save Israel from Pharaoh's wicked grip. However, after the salvation came the training to take Israel through the fellowship of His suffering. They had known His power to save, but the Father also needed to know them by bringing them into the place of intimate fellowship. He has often chosen the line of suffering and chastisement to prove and to know us.

Here, the Bible recorded a bit of the action for our learning: "The Lord your God led you all the way these forty years in the wilderness, to humble you and test you, to know what was in your heart, whether you would keep His commandments or not. So He humbled you, allowed you to hunger, and fed you with manna which you did not know nor did your fathers know, that He might make you know that man shall not live by bread alone; but man lives by every word that proceeds from the mouth of the Lord. Your garments did not wear out on you, nor did your foot swell these forty years. You should know in your heart that as a man chastens his son, so the Lord your God chastens you" (Deut 8:2-5, NKJV). How about that?

Moses had opportunity to become the next Pharaoh, but he chose the path of the fellowship of Christ's sufferings. The Bible recorded that "Moses, when he became of age, refused to be called the son of Pharaoh's daughter, choosing rather to suffer affliction with the people of God than to enjoy the passing pleasures of sin, esteeming the reproach of Christ greater riches than the treasures in Egypt; for he looked to the reward" (Heb 11:24-26, NKJV). The moment God's anointing came upon David to become the next king of Israel after Saul, David started the school of knowing the fellowship of His suffering. King Saul pursued him till his last breath. Day and night, he sought his life to kill him, but nobody dies in this school until Father is through with the training. What else can I say?

The list is endless of men and women who walked with God through the school of the fellowship of His sufferings. This was said of some unnamed heroes of faith, "they were tortured, not accepting deliverance, that they might obtain a better resurrection. Still others had trials of mocking and scourging, yes, and of chains and imprisonment. They were stoned, they were sawn in two, were tempted, and were slain with the sword. They wandered about in sheepskins and goatskins, being destitute, afflicted, tormented, of whom the world was not worthy. They wandered in deserts and mountains, in dens and caves of the earth" (Heb 11:35-38, NKJV). Think about it brethren; if it is the same heaven that these great saints laboured for that we are preparing to enter, there is only one way. We must go beyond the head, goody-goody knowledge of God and enter into the fellowship of His suffering.

In a bid to avoid knowing the fellowship of Christ's suffering, the enemy crept in unawares teaching us that Christians will be taken away and be raptured before the tribulation. Today the church is confused in the presence of obvious sufferings and all manner of tribulations going on while we are still waiting for the rapture. This has ended up raising Christians in our time who are never ready to do the end-time battle against the perilous spirit of the many antichrists. We are not ready to stand up for Jesus in the face of all the antichristian activities of our time. All over the world today, so much tribulation is going on, Christians are being tortured and killed. It all began since our Lord Christ ascended up on high and will continue in greater dimension until He comes for the elect (Matt.24:21,22).

We must restore those teachings and begin to seek the knowledge of the fellowship of His suffering. It yields great advantages that nothing else can impact. The experience is not meant to sink us, but to build us. It is also pertinent to know that God is always there to supply grace in abundance to see us through any suffering that He allows. The scripture is very clear that God waits for us at the end of every fellowship of His suffering to do some new things. "The God of all grace, who hath called us unto his eternal glory by Christ Jesus, after that ye have suffered a while, make you perfect, stablish, strengthen, settle you" (1 Peter 5:10).

We can therefore deduce from this scripture that a certain level of perfection that we need to come to, to announce us before God and the great cloud of witnesses can only be attained after graduating from a divinely arranged fellowship of His suffering. If we boycott it by whatever means, we aren't going to come to that perfection. We discover further that we can never have our feet established on this rough and rugged way to eternal life until we know and embrace the fellowship of His suffering. The Bible also makes it clear here that after passing through the fellowship of His suffering, God will strengthen us. This Christian race requires a lot of spiritual strength to stand against the wiles of the devil. Such strength is not made available to those who are not ready to know the fellowship of Christ's suffering. The Lord said that we gain strength after seasons of suffering as a Christian. Again, the Lord promises to settle us after allowing us go through any suffering for His name's sake.

Now, we discover the reason the scripture admonished us on what should be our attitude to suffering as

Christians: "Dear friends, don't be surprised at the fiery trials you are going through, as if something strange thing were happening to you. Instead, be very glad— for these trials make you partners with Christ in His suffering, so that you will have the wonderful joy of seeing His glory when it is revealed to all the world" (1 Peter 4:12-13, NLT). Wow! So we see that identifying with Christ's suffering brings us into true partnership with our Lord Jesus Christ. It takes us into the place of intimacy with our Lord.

The one reason any Christian would be told by the Lord, "I don't know you" on the Day of Judgment is simply because we never came into partnership relationship with Him. We cannot be brought into a place of partnership with the Lord and be denied by Him. Entering into the fellowship of His suffering becomes inevitable, seeing the glory that comes along with it. The glory that follows after the suffering with Christ can never be compared with whatever we lost. Even our Master and Lord Jesus Christ learnt obedience to God our Father "through the things which He suffered", while He walked the earth (Heb. 5:8). Yet, we have our choice to make as always. God our Father has never imposed His will on us. However, every choice we make comes with its sure reward or consequences. "If we suffer, we shall also reign with him: if we deny him, he also will deny us" (2 Tim 2:12).

7
KNOWING HIS DYING

*"...we were joined with Christ Jesus, in his death...;
we died and were buried with Christ..."*
(Rom 6:3-4, NLT)

The whole essence of knowing and entering into the fellowship of Christ's suffering is for us to be made conformable unto His death. Hear the words of Paul the Apostle once again. "I want to suffer with him, sharing in his death" (Phil 3:10, NLT). After our salvation comes the real life, dying with Christ. The ultimate hope of believers in Christ is the resurrection to a new life here, and everlasting life after. There can never be a resurrection without dying first. If we remain afraid of knowing the fellowship of Christ's suffering, we will never be prepared to share in His death, and ultimately His resurrection.

Until we are joined with Christ Jesus in His death and

burial, we can never be known of Him. The Bible text in this chapter explains that what happens when we surrender our 'life' to Christ is more than the physical answering of an altar call and the confession of sins. The scriptural verse says that at salvation "…we were joined with Christ Jesus, in his death…; we died and were buried with Christ…" (Rom 6:3-4, NLT). This is the greatest mystery of our time. Though living, yet dead and buried. The mortal man can never understand this mystery. The celebration of the simplicity of the salvation experience; the marvelous grace and joy of salvation that accompanies it, will never allow us know the price of our redemption. If we stop on that periphery, we are not going to be able fulfil the demands of the new life. The obvious is that we will not be able to go far with the Lord.

The only people that will enjoy this great experience of salvation are those who will go further to seek to know, like Paul the Apostle desired, to "follow after, if that I (we) may apprehend that for which also I (we have been) am apprehended of Christ Jesus" (Phil 3:12). The salvation experience is a complete reversal of what happened when man sinned against God in the

Garden of Eden. Remember that God told Adam that the day you eat of the fruit in the midst of the garden, you will surely die (Gen.2:17). So, when man disobeyed God, the spirit man died, while the flesh lived on. The flesh which by nature cannot fathom the things of God took over control of the soul of man. Great tragedy! The Spirit of God in man which should give the flesh direction in line with God's will went dead. So, the devil took over the driving of the flesh to fulfil his own will.

Salvation is a transformation. It is all about putting the flesh to death, and restoring life and control again to the spirit man. Being an earthen vessel and having enjoyed control over the soul of man, the flesh does not want to hear about suffering and dying. This is however what the salvation experience is designed to accomplish in our lives. This is the reason we enter into an internal warfare the moment we embrace the word of salvation. This internal conflict is stated thus: "The sinful nature (the flesh) wants to do evil, which is just the opposite of what the Spirit wants. And the Spirit gives us desires that are the opposite of what the sinful nature desires. These two forces are constantly fighting each other, so you are not free to carry out the things that you would"

(Gal 5:17, NLT).

Salvation is a conscious effort to allow the Spirit of God to mortify, to put to death the deeds of the flesh (Rom.8:13). We can never be genuine Christians for as long as we continue to indulge in everything that keep gratifying the fleshly nature. Therefore, the scripture says, "put to death your members which are on the earth: fornication, uncleanness, passion, evil desire, and covetousness, which is idolatry" (Col.3:5, NKJV). Like Paul the Apostle and the early Christians, every believer in Christ must make the choice willingly to die daily (1 Cor.15:31). The flesh is earthly, and does not want the soul of man to cooperate with the Spirit of God.

Brethren, the flesh does not get born again. Rather our spirit man does, and begins to enforce control of the activities of the flesh. We must know that the body was created to fulfil the earthly purpose for which the Father made it. So unless the Spirit of God uses our bodies, we can never fulfil divine purpose. This flesh will definitely return to the mother earth without regrets one day, because the body was formed from the earth. Irrespective of colour, race, status, or belief, it will definitely expire here, while the soul, the real man returns to God to give account how we lived here on earth.

So, we discover that when we try to avoid suffering and dying with Christ we delude ourselves, because this flesh will definitely expire and die one day. If we refuse to die to the flesh by choice and yield control to the Spirit of God, we will still die someday, but regrettably will lose our soul to the eternal, burning lake of fire. This is what the Bible calls the second death, which is the eternal consequence of refusing to identify with the death of our Lord and Saviour Jesus Christ (Rev.21:8). He told us while He was here on earth that when we try to save our life, by avoiding everything that identifies us with His death, we will lose it at last. "For whosoever would save his life will lose it, but whosoever loses his life for my sake will save it" (Luke 9:24, ESV).

The Bible did not deceive us in this matter. Our Lord Jesus Christ died, leaving us an example that we should follow, but here we are, running away from what we are called to be part of. Our salvation opens the gateway and releases to us the grace to follow Jesus to the place of identifying with His death. This is clearly demonstrated by the experience of baptism after our repentance. Jesus Christ told the disciples, "Go into all the world and proclaim the gospel to the whole creation. Whoever believes and is baptized will be saved, but whoever does not believe will be condemned" (Mark 16:15-17, ESV).

One might be wondering, "what's the need for baptism after surrendering my life to Christ?" I wondered for a while after I repented and got converted until the Lord ministered to me. If baptism must accompany our repentance before our salvation is complete, then baptism is more than a religious sacrament as we seem to have reduced it to in our time. Baptism is a physical demonstration of our salvation experience. If our salvation does not take us to the place of true mortification of this flesh, and take us deep down the grave with our Lord Jesus, it is doubtful what we are running with. Here is how Paul the apostle explained the mystery of baptism.

"Do you not know that all of us who have been baptized into Christ Jesus were baptized into his death? We were buried therefore with him by baptism into death, in order that, just as Christ was raised from the dead by the glory of the Father, we too might walk in newness of life. For if we have been united with Him in a death like His, we shall certainly be united with him in a resurrection like His. We know that our old self was crucified with Him in order that the body of sin might be brought to nothing, so that we would no longer be enslaved to sin. For one who has died has been set free from sin. Now if we have died with Christ, we believe that we will also live with him" (Rom 6:3-8, ESV).

Brethren, the scripture cannot be broken. The flesh does not want to die. He wants to remain in charge over our spirit man, even after we have repented and surrendered our lives to Christ. Our salvation should not stop at the gate of the joy of salvation. We should not stop at the joy gate of liberation from the bondage of sin and sicknesses. Do not allow the devil engage you with the miracles of prosperity and all the breakthroughs that come with the grace of salvation. Above all, we should not allow the messengers that were sent or used to lead us to the only Way, the Truth and the Life to hold or halt our journey to God. They are only messengers. They might be angels; they are not the Christ. Follow through until you meet Christ. Don't stop at any Abraham's gate as your father. Refuse to move from one level of religious bondage to a higher one.

The devil is ready to give us anything to stop us from going on to the place of dying daily with Christ Jesus. He did it to the first Adam, he succeeded. He offered our Lord Jesus Christ (the second Adam), the whole world to stop Him from going the way of the cross. Praise God, he failed. If we make up our minds to follow through to know His salvation; know His suffering till we come to the place of His death, we will then be joined in His resurrection.

We are meant to live the resurrected lives here after our repentance and salvation from sin. Only then shall we be made ready to join in the resurrection unto eternal life. Practically explaining his own experience, Paul the Apostle said, "I have been crucified with Christ; it is no longer I who live, but Christ lives in me; and the life which I now live in the flesh I live by faith in the Son of God, who loved me and gave Himself for me" (Gal

2:20, NKJV). Until the sinful nature and its lusts is put to death and buried with Christ, we can never arise in newness of life. The Christian life therefore, becomes an impossibility for as long as we refuse to accept and yield willingly to die with Christ. This is what the message of baptism is all about. When we only observe the baptismal doctrine as a religious sacrament without practically demonstrating identification with Christ's death, burial and the new life, we will be disappointed on the day of eternal resurrection. This is the reason people will be told, 'Depart, I never knew you'.

8
KNOWING HIS RESURRECTION

"That I may know the power of His resurrection ...if, by any means, I may attain to the resurrection from the dead" (Phil 3:10-11, NKJV)

Great people of God, it feels so exciting to state without mincing words at this juncture that our Lord Jesus Christ came to bring us back to life. We were dead in trespasses and became helpless as it were until our Lord Jesus Christ came to save us. Mankind lost the nature of God and took on the nature of the devil after disobeying God in the Garden of Eden. Man became an embodiment of darkness, wickedness and evil. It was only the resurrection power, demonstrated by our Lord Jesus Christ that raised us up from the body of this death. Until we know this resurrection power, we can never be able to live the new life.

Paul the Apostle could not fathom this great turn around; from the depth of wickedness to a glorious life. As he labored under the helpless bondage of this sinful nature, he once cried out, "Oh, what a miserable person I am! Who will free me from this life that is dominated by sin and death? Thank God! The answer is in Jesus Christ our Lord" (Rom 7:24-25, NLT). It is an incredible work, people! No other word could well describe the great experience of salvation from the works of darkness than the power of resurrection.

This power is better experienced than told. As a matter of fact, it is meant to be experienced, and not to be told as Bible stories. The death and resurrection of Jesus has every feature and qualification to make a great, world class movie or story book. In fact, it is a thriller. It is very easy to be carried away with the 'liquid content only'. In those days when drinks and wines were produced in breakable bottle containers, the advertisers of those drinks would always end the advert with the remark, "liquid content only". The essence is to convince prospective buyers that what they are advertising and selling is the liquid content only. So, the bottles and containers are returnable after enjoying your drink.

What are we saying here?

It is very easy to keep singing our beautiful songs of the amazing, saving grace of our Lord Jesus Christ which is like the liquid content only of all that our Lord came to do for us. We must be ready to eat His flesh and drink His blood. Jesus told the multitude that followed him because of physical bread: "I tell you the truth, unless you eat the flesh of the Son of Man and drink his blood, you cannot have eternal life within you. But anyone who eats my flesh and drinks my blood has eternal life, and I will raise that person at the last day. For my flesh is true food, and my blood is true drink. Anyone who eats my flesh and drinks my blood remains in me, and I in him" (John 6:53-56, NLT). What a statement? It didn't make sense to that multitude. This wasn't what they bargained for.

They all turned back from following the Lord, saying, "This is very hard to understand. How can anyone accept it?" (John 6:60, NLT). Do we blame them? The man in the flesh can never understand the resurrected life. This veil has remained till today. All the charismatic demonstration of the gifts that we do today, not rooted in the new life will not carry us far. As long as we keep halting and rejecting every thorn sent from God to buffet our flesh daily, we can never rise above the carnal demands of the flesh. The Christian life is a resurrected life; it is an entirely new life, not just a changed life. The resurrected life is only made possible after death and burial; that is, putting to death the deeds of the flesh. So that, "just as Christ was raised from the dead by the glory of the Father, we too might walk in newness of life. For if we have been united with him in a death like His, we shall certainly be united with Him in a resurrection like His" (Rom.6:4,5).

This is the wonder of all ages. We are called to know the power of His resurrection. It is the knowledge of this power that sustains us in the new birth experience. It is the knowledge of this resurrection power that makes believers in Christ stand strong in the face of every fiery dart of the wicked. Even before the coming of our Lord Jesus Christ, those that ever did exploits in the name of the Lord believed so much in this power. They believed in the resurrection power and lived valiantly in the hope of its manifestation. Though, they did not live to see the practical consummation of the prophecies of the Lord's death and resurrection, the belief and hope kept them burning.

Our Lord Jesus Christ made reference to those great men of faith when challenging the disciples in one of His teachings thus: "I tell you the truth, many prophets and righteous people longed to see what you see, but they didn't see it. And they longed to hear what you hear, but they didn't hear it" (Matt 13:17, NLT). Shadrach, Meshach and Abednego did not yield to the death threat of King Nebuchadnezzar as he roared, "I will give you one more chance to bow down and worship the statue I have made when you hear the sound of the musical instruments. But if you refuse, you will be thrown immediately into the blazing furnace. And then what god will be able to rescue you from my power?" (Dan.3:15, NLT)

Look at their fearless response: Shadrach, Meshach, and Abednego replied, "O Nebuchadnezzar, we do not need to defend ourselves before you. If we are thrown into the blazing furnace, the God whom we serve is able to save us. He will rescue us from your power, Your Majesty. But even if he doesn't, we want to make it clear to you, Your Majesty, that we will never serve your gods or worship the gold statue you have set up" (Dan.3:16-18, NLT). Only the strong knowledge and belief in the power of resurrection could have given them such a courage. It was the strength of their faith that moved heaven and brought Jesus (the Son of man) into the fiery furnace.

The king and his army of mockers were stunned at the demonstration of the power of resurrection. "Look!" he answered, "I see four men loose, walking in the midst of the fire; and they are not hurt, and the form of the fourth is like the Son of God" (Dan.3:25, NKJV). It is so thrilling to live above the flesh. It is so wonderful to allow God put this flesh to death, so we can be raised again by God Himself. We must begin to enforce the fear of God and the supremacy of heaven in our generation through our uncompromising commitment to the course of heaven.

This can only be made possible by knowing and living the resurrected life. Imagine the 'almighty king Nebuchadnezzar' shaking like a reed as he came as close as he could to the door of the flaming furnace and shouted: "Shadrach, Meshach, and Abednego, servants of the Most High God, come out! Come here! So Shadrach, Meshach, and Abednego stepped out of the fire. Then the high officers, officials, governors, and advisers crowded around them and saw that the fire had not touched them. Not a hair on their heads was singed, and their clothing was not scorched. They didn't even smell of smoke!" (Dan.3:26-27, NLT).

You can't beat the power of resurrection. The resurrected life is the real kingdom life; it is bringing down heaven's life to bear upon the lives of men. You will agree with me that you cannot bring heaven down here, and the Lord will tell you, "Depart, I never knew you," on the day of reckoning. Our greatest problem today is that we only sing and celebrate the religious, historical aspect of the resurrection, while denying the power therein. Paul, the Apostle couldn't make that mistake as he sought to know the power of His resurrection. Writing to the Colossian Church, he admonished us saying, "Since you have been raised to new life with Christ, set your sights on the realities of heaven, where Christ sits in the place of honor at God's right hand. Think about the things of heaven, not the things of earth. For you died to this life, and your real life is hidden with Christ in God. And when Christ, who is your life, is revealed to the whole world, you will share in all His glory" (Col.3:1-4, NLT).

We can never be afraid of what the judgment will be for us when we have already lost our lives in Him while on earth. The Christian life will remain an impossibility for the mortal man until we die to self, and begin to live in Him, move and have our being in Him alone (Acts 17:28). The early Church stood out for everything that Christ represented, including the cross. Persecution, perils, nakedness, hunger and all forms of tribulations of life were hard on them, but none of those things could stop or separate them from the love of Christ. Those things only helped to mortify their flesh, and set their spirit man aglow for heaven. Today, the end time Church seems to have tactfully avoided all those hard trials through a subtle compromise with the world.

A common parlance says, "We cannot eat our cake and have it." The risen life of Christ cannot be lived by those who refuse to share in the death, burial, and resurrection of Christ. If we deny Him, He remains faithful. If we want to leave this world like the Heroes of faith, who knew where they were going from here while wearing this earthen vessel, then we must seek to know and live in the power of resurrection. Paul the Apostle who sought earnestly to know the power of His resurrection left us with this challenge before he died, "For I am already being poured out as a drink offering, and the time of my departure is at hand. I have fought the good fight, I have finished the race, I have kept the faith. Finally, there is laid up for me the crown of righteousness, which the Lord, the righteous Judge, will give to me on that Day, and not to me only but also to all who have loved His appearing" (2 Tim 4:6-8, NLT).

So, the list of saints who will make it to heaven is endless. We can all put our names on the list. The qualification is to seek to know and to live in the power of His resurrection daily. Those who love and are waiting for His appearing are those that are living in the new and resurrected life already. No believer in Christ who identified with Christ in His death and resurrection here will be denied by the Lord when He sits to judge the whole world. When the Lord will appear at the sound of the trumpet, this resurrection connection will wake even the dead in Christ.

I love the way the Bible puts it: "But I do not want you to be ignorant, brethren, concerning those who have fallen asleep, lest you sorrow as others who have no hope. For if we believe that Jesus died and rose again, even so God will bring with Him those who sleep in Jesus. For this we say to you by the word of the Lord, that we who are alive and remain until the coming of the Lord will by no means precede those who are asleep. For the Lord Himself will descend from heaven with a shout, with the voice of an archangel, and with the trumpet of God. And the dead in Christ will rise first. Then we who are alive and remain shall be caught up together with them in the clouds to meet the Lord in the air. And thus, we shall always be with the Lord" (1 Thess. 4:13-17, NKJV).

We discover that the word, 'sleep' was used, instead of 'death' for those believers who die in Christ. Meaning that those who die in Christ Jesus only sleep, waiting for the day when Christ who is their life, would come to wake them up (John 11:25,26). Another very striking statement here is that those believers who would remain alive at the Lord's coming and those who were dead in Christ will hear the trumpet sound at the same time and will arise to meet with the Lord at the same time. Those who live and those who died all have the same spirit quickening power working in the same capacity. Wow! Incredible, Awesome Glory!

Meanwhile, those who are alive, physically sound and healthy, but not alive in Christ Jesus, will not even hear this awakening, trumpet sound; not to talk of arising to meet with the Lord. The difference is very clear. The connection point is the power of resurrection. When we are saved from sin, and the grip of hell, we should allow the Lord to take us through the only way that leads home, that is the way of the Cross. The Cross will crush the flesh and give us the resurrected, new life in Christ Jesus. We cannot go this way and get disappointed at the judgment throne.

9
KNOWING HIS PRESENCE

"...the natural man does not receive the things of the Spirit of God ...nor can he know them, because they are spiritually discerned." (1 Cor 2:14, NKJV).

Sitting daily under the school of the Spirit of God to learn the spirit-life, is what we can never avoid if we must know and relate with God intimately as our Father. Suffice it to say here that the new life in Christ goes beyond a moral change of character. It is more than changing from an orthodox church to a Pentecostal church. So many people end up in the local church or a religious organization after our encounter with the Lord Jesus Christ. In the course of time, we end up becoming very good fans of the pastor/bishop-leader. At best, our lives easily get blended and patterned after the church beliefs and dogmas, and less after Christ. Consequently, we find ourselves living a double standard life after proclaiming salvation from sin. We become different people in the church and different people all together in the office, at home or any other environment where there is no church member to fault our actions.

This is very typical of the Jewish, Scribes and Pharisees lifestyle. The Pharisees were more conscious of the presence of human beings than they were of God's presence. The reason was because at the dispensation of the law, one is presumed to be innocent until you are caught in the very act, or at the mouth of two or three witnesses. So, they ended up becoming religious robots and hypocrites, having a form of godliness, but denying the power thereof (2 Tim.3:5). The law could only produce religious idols out of mortal men, rather than spirit filled men. At that level of religious life, it became difficult to convince the Pharisees of life in the spirit. Hence they contended with the Lord Jesus Christ until they killed Him in 'defense of God'.

This is a very dangerous state to come to as a Christian. Many of us are still sitting today where the Pharisees sat; learning all the tongue-speaking, customized religious languages and psalms till we have become religious idols. This was why our Lord Jesus Christ instructed

His disciples before His ascension saying, "You are witnesses of all these things. And now I will send the Holy Spirit, just as my Father promised. But stay here in the city until the Holy Spirit comes and fills you with power from heaven" (Luke 24:48-49, NLT). After dying and resurrecting with Christ we can only become spirit-beings, and no more, unless if we never died. Nobody dies and rises up as a mortal human being.

The New life in Christ Jesus is only made possible because our spirit-man with which we related with God before the failure comes alive again. Remember that man died after disobeying God by eating the forbidden fruit. In the new life, we are going to begin to relate with God again who is Spirit. Since the failure of man, God has continued to seek for men who will begin to worship Him again in spirit and in truth (John 4:23,24). In other words, God has been hungry for true fellowship with man which was only made possible then because the spirit-man was alive and flowed freely with the mind of God. But here we are, having lived all our years under the control of the flesh before we encountered Christ; it is definitely not going to be a day's job.

The new birth implies a brand new life, not just a

changed life. It means we are now born in the spirit; thereby making it possible again to begin to relate with God. The scripture asks, "Who can know the Lord's thoughts? Who knows enough to teach him? But we understand these things, for we have the mind of Christ" (1 Cor.2:16, NLT). If Paul the Apostle left us to answer the questions on the 'A' part of that scriptural verse, we could have boldly answered, 'Nobody can know the mind of God'. Fortunately, Paul didn't leave that question open ended. He made an exemption on the part 'B' saying, "but we understand these things, for we have the mind of Christ". Halleluya! What a wonderful privilege!

However, this understanding of spiritual things or the mind of God does not come automatically in one experience. Every new move requires a great deal of training if we must grow in it. Therefore, this new birth experience requires a continual learning and development of our spiritual sensory nerves until we are going to be able to begin to discern God's presence in our daily activities. Any moment we fail to do this, the devil takes undue advantage and deceives us. This is a life-time training. As new born babies in the spirit-life,

Peter the elder advised that drinking the sincere milk of the word of God daily will afford us the opportunity to learn and develop our spiritual sensory nerves (1 Pet.2:2).

This purposeful commitment to learning daily under the school of the Spirit will make it possible for us to begin to understand and respond accurately to every nudge of the Spirit of God. This will also begin to make God's presence real around us at all times. This is exactly what the person of the Holy Spirit came to teach and to inculcate in us, believers in Christ Jesus. Our Lord Jesus Christ called him our Teacher and our Comforter. Jesus said that it is expedient that He goes away from the earth, so that the Holy Spirit takes over the stage to complete the total work of the final redemption of man (John 16:7). It becomes evidently clear here that the Holy Spirit is the Spirit of Christ at work in man. Any man who desires to live for Christ today must take the personality of the Holy Spirit as seriously as the disciples did with our Lord Jesus Christ while he walked the earth.

We must take good advantage of the teaching ministry

of the Holy Spirit, to allow Him train and develop our spirit-man. When He is through with us, the invisibility of God will be made visible to us. By the time He is through with us, we should be able to confess like the early apostles: "that...which we have heard, which we have seen with our eyes, which we have looked upon, and our hands have handled, concerning the Word of life; ... that which we have seen and heard we declare to you, that you also may have fellowship with us; and truly our fellowship is with the Father and with His Son Jesus Christ" (1 John 1:1-3, NKJV). Don't be deceived to think that Apostle John made those comments because they were with the Lord Jesus physically when He was here. Not at all.

Think about this. It couldn't have been the same apostles that fled when the Lord Jesus Christ was arrested that could be saying this. Certainly not the same apostles that were telling Jesus, "We have no idea where You are going, so how can we know the way?" (John 14:5, NLT). Obviously not the same apostles that our Lord Jesus Christ told in disappointment: "Have I been with you so long, and yet you have not known Me"? (John 14:9, NKJV). The apostles that the

Lord Jesus left behind were wishy-washy, fearful, self-seeking, faithless, religious folks. They were turned to something else by the great ministry of the Holy Spirit. The Lord Jesus depended so much on the Holy Spirit to perfect all the deficiencies of these apostles, and He did a perfect work. (John 16:12-14).

Brethren, what we cannot see, we cannot possess. Fellowship with an invisible God that you cannot see nor feel is an impossibility. We must be joking to be fellowshipping with a Spirit when we don't understand His language and moves. This, unfortunately is the state of so many 'so called' believers today. Until we begin to be very conscious of God's visible presence around us through His Spirit daily, we will never be genuine Christians. The greatest thing limiting man from relating with God is the absence of the consciousness of the reality of God's presence around us. The constant awareness of the presence of God will take away the illusion of relating with a God that we cannot see.

Warning the church against the deceptions of the antichrists, John the Beloved wrote, "I am writing these things to warn you about those who want to lead you astray. But you have received the Holy Spirit, and He lives within you, so you don't need anyone to teach you what is true. For the Spirit teaches you everything you need to know, and what He teaches is true; it is not a lie. So, just as He has taught you, remain in fellowship with Christ; living as Children of God. And now, dear children, remain in fellowship with Christ so that when He returns, you will be full of courage and not shrink back from Him in shame" (1 John 2:26-28).

What do we discover here, my brethren? It becomes very clear that the only thing that will save us the embarrassing, shameful judgment, "Depart, I never knew you" is to enter into a constant, living fellowship with God. It is only through the agency of the person of the Holy Spirit alone that this fellowship with God could be made possible. The natural man does not and can never understand the things of the Spirit, because they are spiritually discerned. Even if you were a professor in Christian religious studies before you got born again, you must trash all that mental knowledge of God and surrender to the school of the Spirit. This was the reason our Lord Jesus Christ did not mince words as He spoke to High priest Nicodemus, "I tell you the truth, unless you are born again, you cannot see the Kingdom of God" (John 3:3 NLT). This statement didn't make sense to this reputable, Jewish, religious leader. He quickly exclaimed to Jesus, "What do you mean? How can an old man go back into his mother's womb and be born again?" (John 3:4, NLT).

Just as in every other facet of learning in life, the more we learn and do well at every stage or level, the more the teacher feels confident to take us deeper. In the same parlance, one can only make progress in understanding the things of the Spirit when we begin to put into practice the little we learn in the school of the Spirit from one level to another. There are depths of spirit life we can never reach until we die to the flesh. We must therefore be in a hurry to learn and practice what we've learnt if we must make any progress. Unfortunately, this is far from our attitude to spiritual things today. We have so many Nicodemus-bishops and General Overseers who have refused to submit to the teaching ministry of the Holy Spirit. So many young converts do not want to humbly submit to the Holy Spirit to train and develop their spirit man.

We must learn from the school of the Spirit to the point that we can discern our Lord's voice clearly even in the midst of all dissenting voices, no matter how strong those dissenting voices are. We must get so acquainted with the soft, sweet voice of the Spirit of God to be able to enjoy the fellowship of the Father, Son and the Holy Spirit. In a world that hates God, using all manner of channels to promote negative, evil voices; employing every technological means to promote the evil agenda of the antichrist, we need to be able to discern God's voice to withstand their negative tide. In the midst of so many false, heretic teachers of 'another gospel', who have crept in unawares, we need the help of the Holy Spirit to be able to test every spirit whether they be of God (1 John 4:1).

We must continue to learn until we become fully conscious of God's presence through His Spirit. "For as many as are led by the Spirit of God, these are sons of God. The Spirit Himself bears witness with our spirit that we are children of God" (Rom 8:14,16, NKJV). Even in our prayers, we cannot pray in line with God's will unless we receive help from the Holy Spirit. God has made Himself visible to us, but we can only see

Him through the eyes of our spirit. When we live in full consciousness of His presence, we will never miss it. God reveals things to us by His Spirit. For His Spirit searches out everything and shows us God's deep secrets. No one can know a person's thoughts except that person's own spirit, and no one can know God's thoughts except God's own Spirit. And we have received God's Spirit (not the world's spirit), so we can know the wonderful things God has freely given us" (1 Cor 2:10-12). This is what marks us out as Christians.

10
KNOWING HIS APPEARING

"The crown of righteousness, awaits all who eagerly look forward to his appearing. (2 Tim 4:8, NLT)

The greatest and most exciting experience that keeps the hope of every Christian alive is the second coming of our Lord Jesus Christ to take us away from this world. This is the rallying point of the whole essence of becoming a Christian. The joy of meeting with the personality of the Triune God the Father, the Son and the Holy Spirit is the ultimate expectation of every believer in Christ Jesus. The return of the kingdom that was lost by man in Eden, and the total restoration of all that man lost in relationship with God in Eden is what every true believer in Christ is eagerly waiting for today.

While the apostles gazed intently into the heavens in utter dismay as our Lord Jesus Christ ascended up into the heavens, "Behold, two men in white clothing stood beside them, and said unto them, " Men of Galilee, why do you stand looking into the sky? This Jesus, who has been taken up from you into heaven, will come in just the same way as you have watched Him go into heaven" (Acts 1:10-11). What a great consolation! What a relief it brought to their minds! The liveliness of this hope took them all to the Upper Room, and kept them all in one accord as they waited patiently for the promise of the Father.

When the Holy Spirit descended, the Bible testified that they were all in one accord, and were all filled with the Holy Spirit. The power of the hope of His second appearing kept them alive and strong in the faith. They continued in the strength of this hope even after the Holy Spirit came upon their lives. They greeted one another in an expression of this hope: 'Maranatha', meaning 'our Lord cometh'. The hope of His coming again was the rallying point of the unity of the early church. Even when they were all scattered abroad by persecution, this hope sustained them wherever they found themselves. The Bible testified that they stood and rejoiced in hope of the glory (Rom.5:2).

Wonderful hope!

The hope of Christ's second coming breeds in every believer the faith and patience desired to inherit the promised kingdom (Heb.6:12). The hope of His appearing keeps us in sweet Communion with the Spirit of God which He left for us as a guarantee that He is coming again for us. This mortal body will soon put on immortality, conquering the flesh finally (2 Cor.5:4,5). Halleluya! We are expected to draw from the well of this hope till the wake of eternity. This is what brings us naturally into the place of intimacy with God. The more we draw from this well, the more He reveals more of what eternity holds for every believer. It is in the strength of this grace that we rejoice even in the time of troubles, trials and tribulations of this age.

At the end of the Island of Patmos revelation experience, these were great, reassuring words to John the Beloved for all saints, "Yes, I'm on my way! I'll be there soon! I'm bringing my payroll with me. I'll pay all people in full for their life's work. I'm A to Z, the First and the Final, Beginning and Conclusion. He who testifies to all these things says it again: "I'm on my way! I'll be there soon!" (Rev 22:12-13,20, THE MESSAGE BIBLE). The excitement of the expectation of His coming spurred the urgent response from John, "Yes! Come, Master Jesus!" Every true believer should be able to develop such an intimate relationship with God to be able to say at every point in time, "Yes, come Lord Jesus, even now".

The believer in Christ Jesus must be unwavering in focusing on the coming kingdom. It remains the pivot of the call to repentance. John the Baptist preached it pointedly, "Repent of your sins and turn to God, for the Kingdom of Heaven is near" (Matt 3:2, NLT). The ministration of our Lord Jesus Christ emphasized the coming kingdom the moment He started His earthly ministry. Hear Him, "Repent of your sins and turn to God, for the Kingdom of Heaven is near" (Matt 4:17, NLT). As Pastor Nicodemus came by night with his praise flatteries, the Lord did not waste time to enjoy the praises as he quickly told him, "I tell you the truth, unless you are born again, you cannot see the Kingdom of God" (John 3:3, NLT). Paul the apostle now nailed it down clearly saying, "If our hope in Christ is only for this life, we are more to be pitied than anyone in the world" (1 Cor 15:19, NLT). What else can I say?

Brethren we can now easily discover at this point that most of our acclaimed repentance is not real. Every true repentance must be spurred on by a burning desire for the kingdom of God. Our desire for miracles, healing, prosperity and material breakthroughs are good and can draw us to God but should not deceive us as if it means repentance. It is easy to think that when those prayers are answered out of God's mercies, it means we have repented. Until we begin to seek the kingdom of God and His righteousness, our claim of repentance is very doubtful. This the reason why so many do not go far in the faith.

Even when we are truly born again, the devil will use every means to try to steal from our heart the desire for His appearance. The only thing that can sustain the faith of a poor, suffering child of God is the hope of His appearance. The only grace that can save the rich Christian brother or sister from becoming another 'rich fool' (Luke 12:20,21) is the great expectation of our heavenly home. His glorious appearance is the rallying point of the rich and the poor believers, the strong and the weak believers, the bishops and the ordinary church members. This hope is our unifying force, brethren. Perhaps, the reason for the disunity and multiplication of churches and worship centers today could be traceable to the pursuit of other insatiable interests, at the negligence of the coming of our Lord Jesus Christ. Think about it. If we are all headed for the same direction and have the same focus, we should have understanding among ourselves.

Getting lost in enjoyment of the lusts of the flesh, the eyes and the pride of life is unavoidable when we fail to seek and to expect His appearance. The moment the devil succeeds in taking our focus away from this great expectation of the appearance of our Lord Jesus Christ Who will take us away from the kingdom of this world to the kingdom of God, we are finished as Christians. This has remained the greatest strategy of the devil in deceiving the world; hiding away from our heart, the imminence of Christ's second coming. Today, the Church that was instituted with the mandate to preach and to pray daily, 'Thy Kingdom come', is rather busy building her own kingdom here on earth. The complete loss of this consciousness that our Lord Jesus Christ is coming again, quickly is one great beast ravaging the Church today.

Our Lord Jesus Christ knew that the temptation to forget His appearance would be strong with the passage of time. He warned us, "A faithful, sensible servant is one to whom the master can give the responsibility of managing his other household servants and feeding them. If the servant thinks, 'My master won't be back for a while,' and he begins to beat the other servants, partying, and getting drunk, the master will return unannounced and unexpected, and he will cut the servant in pieces and banish him with the unfaithful" (Luke 12:42,45-46, NLT). The temptation to join the world is strong the moment we lose thought of His appearance. Demas, a companion of Paul, the Apostle left him the moment his love for the present world beclouded his love for the coming kingdom (2 Tim.4:10). It is most likely that the people being told 'Depart, I never knew you' by the Lord, were servants of God who lost their focus at one point of their pilgrim journey just like Demas.

Though, our Lord could not tell the Church the specific

time of His appearing to take the saints home, every information needed to keep track was released to us in form of signs. Signs are often used by professionals in different fields of learning. Every facet of life, spiritual and physical, skilled and unskilled, financial, literary, medical, technical, military, judiciary and so on, all have peculiar signs known to only those who belong to those groups. It is only those who go deep in the knowledge of such signs that will understand the usage at every point in time.

In the same vein, Christians are expected to be spiritually knowledgeable enough to be able to decode the sign language of the spirit world. This includes the signs of His second coming. The unfolding of the events surrounding Christ's second appearance makes the Christian journey very adventurous and interesting. It is in the place of intimate relationship with God that we begin to get acquainted with the signs of His second coming. Those who remain at the peripheral knowledge of God will never get to know the signs of His appearance. The consequence becomes very obvious. We can never get to be prepared to meet with the Lord smiling, because we never expected

His coming.

The inability to download the signs of the end will make us faint in the Spirit, because it will make serving God look like an unending waiting game. Many have fallen prey already. The expectation of His coming has a way of renewing our strength, in fulfilment of Isaiah's prophecy: "Even the youths shall faint and be weary, And the young men shall utterly fall, But those who wait on the Lord shall renew their strength; They shall mount up with wings like eagles, They shall run and not be weary, they shall walk and not faint" (Isa.40:30-31, NKJV). How about that? It is a natural phenomenon to refuse to give in to weariness when you are pursuing something of great value.

A little wonder in his illustration, Paul the Apostle likened the Christian journey to those who are engaged in a race for a crown. He said that those who are engaged in a race could be many, but only one athlete receives the prize. Therefore, having that at the background of every runner, run in such a way that you may obtain the prize. He went further to buttress the fact that everyone who competes for the prize is temperate in all things, just to obtain a perishable crown, but we are running to win an imperishable crown. "Therefore", he said of himself, "I run thus: not with uncertainty. Thus I fight: not as one who beats the air. But I discipline my body and bring it into subjection, lest, when I have preached to others, I myself should become disqualified" (1 Cor 9:24-27, NKJV). What does that tell us brethren? Running this race with heaven in view, and the crown of life which those who run to the end will receive will definitely keep us on track, and will save us from the judgment, 'Depart, I don't know you'. Only those who run as if they are beating the air will receive that embarrassment.

We live in the perilous times. In the midst of all the storms, tribulations, and the painful distractions of these end times, we can still set right our Christian priorities. Only those who know and expect His appearance will continue to rejoice in the audacity of that hope, no matter the storm. This is our joy today, as prophesied by Isaiah: "O Zion, messenger of good news, shout from the mountaintops! Shout it louder, O Jerusalem. Shout, and do not be afraid. Tell the towns of Judah, "Your God is coming! Yes, the Sovereign Lord is coming in power. He will rule with a powerful arm. See, He brings His reward with Him as He comes" (Isa. 40:9,10 NLT). Who will be next to say, "Come, even now, Lord Jesus."

11
KNOWING HIS JUDGEMENT

They hated knowledge, and chose not to fear the Lord. They rejected my advice and paid no attention when I corrected them. Therefore, they must eat the bitter fruit of living their own way."
(Prov 1:29-31, NLT)

The two sides of God in dealing with man must be understood and taken very seriously by anyone who has anything to do with God. God can be smiling at one person, or a nation, or group of persons, while His anger burns on another person, or group of persons at the same time, without diminishing either part. We must fear this God. When God is happy with a man, His countenance of joy all over you could be so overwhelming and contagious that your enemies will have no choice, but to come and make peace with you. Very incredible! When we find ourselves under such an influence, it is often difficult to believe that His anger can also burn as a consuming fire when we misbehave and fall under His judgment. Paul the Apostle advised that when we receive the grace of salvation, we must serve Him acceptably with reverence and godly fear, "for our God is a consuming fire" (Heb 12:28-29, NKJV).

God's grace and mercy is so amazing, such that we can easily take Him for granted when we don't seek the true knowledge of the Person of God. A careful trace of every person, nation, or generation that ever failed in God's judgment would reveal that almost every one of them took God's mercies and liberality of love for granted. Look at this: "...Does disaster come to a city unless the Lord has planned it? Indeed, the Sovereign Lord never does anything until He reveals His plans to His servants the prophets" (Amos 3:6-7, NLT). We fall into God's judgment when we refuse to heed His warnings through His prophets. God does not delight in His people drifting into disobedience till they get consumed in His wrathful judgment. God's love and mercies endure to the point when it becomes obvious that we have refused to heed His soft and hard warnings.

We must be wise enough to draw a line between God's time of mercies and His severity. We must know Him to that extent. It is dangerous to take things for granted when under the covering of His loving kindness. He warns through His prophet Jeremiah, "Time after time I sent you prophets, who told you, "Turn from your wicked ways, and start doing things right. Stop worshiping other gods so that you might live in peace here in the land I have given to you and your ancestors." But you would not listen to me or obey me. The descendants of Jehonadab son of Recab have obeyed their ancestor completely, but you have refused to listen to me. "Therefore, this is what the Lord God of Heaven's Armies, the God of Israel, says: 'Because you refuse to listen or answer when I call, I will send upon Judah and Jerusalem all the disasters I have threatened" (Jer 35:15-17, NLT). What do we observe from that scripture? Men who hate and despise that knowledge of God that should instill His fear in them, the book of wisdom says that they must eat the bitter fruit of living their own way.

God's countenance can be so sweet and smiling on us for as long as we are with Him. That same countenance can be incredibly wrathful when we turn our back at His warnings. He may not become angry with us at the point of slacking, until we refuse to heed His warnings to return to Him. Every child of God should know Him intimately enough to know when He is smiling at us or when His countenance is sad. That is what makes a relationship flow better. Many of us prefer to stay on the excitement of the knowledge of God's promises and privileges and refuse to know anything about His judgment. It could be dangerous. When we hate the knowledge of the nature of God's judgment, we will hardly know the fear of God. When we don't know the fear of God, the tendency is that we will enter into the problem of undue familiarity with God which will in turn bring contempt. This is the position of so many Christians waiting for the coming of the Lord.

Consider what happened to the anointed cherub Lucifer and the host of angelic beings that got deceived. You will agree with me that the plot of Lucifer to overthrow God was not hatched in one day. It is also obvious that God saw the evil plot from the day Lucifer started nursing that evil plan till His final judgment day. It could be easily predictable that he took the liberality of God's amazing love for granted. He, and the host of deceived angels never expected the judgment would come so hard on him. "How you are fallen from heaven, O Lucifer, son of the morning! How you are cut down to the ground, you who weakened the nations! For you have said in your heart: 'I will ascend into heaven …I will be like the Most High.' Yet you shall be brought down to Sheol, To the lowest depths of the Pit" (Isa 14:12-15, NKJV).

Think about that: his plot was to ascend into heaven, but the judgment brought him to lowest depths of the pit. Remember the already exalted position which he occupied before this evil ambition. The glory he carried, and the beauty he radiated was so much that he was described as 'son of the morning'. All that was lost within a twinkling of an eye. Why? "You were blameless in all you did from the day you were created until the day evil was found in you. You sinned. So I banished you in disgrace from the mountain of God. I expelled you, O mighty guardian, from your place among the stones of fire" (Ezek 28:15-16, NLT). Ah! When you come to know this side of God, it will definitely drive His fear in the innermost part of your heart. God enthrones and dethrones. He kills and makes alive, not just in the past, but in all ages till eternity (1 Sam.2:6). My generation of grace-Christians, beware!

When we seek to know the veracity and uncompromising nature of God's judgment, we will escape the unpleasant judgment of those who take Him for granted. They are the people who will be thinking that the miracles that God used them to perform, or the miracles they received were enough proof that they were children of God. It is people who don't know God's judgment that think that God respects religious titles and all the sacramental specimens that we bear and carry. Those are the people that will be coming to God's judgment seat, telling Him, 'Lord, remember we prophesied in your name, and did many mighty miracles in your name'; and the Bible said, the Lord will tell them, 'I don't know you'. He stands out as a just God with no respect of persons in His judgment.

Oh! Though the early apostles walked with Jesus side by side, through the streets of Galilee, they never allowed that play down on the knowledge of His judgment. Hence Peter drew our ear seriously on this matter: "God did not spare even the angels who sinned. He threw them into hell, in gloomy pits of darkness, where they are being held until the Day of Judgment. And God did not spare the ancient world—except for Noah and the seven others in his family. Noah warned the world of God's righteous judgment. So God protected Noah when he destroyed the world of ungodly people with a vast flood. Later, God condemned the cities of Sodom and Gomorrah and turned them into heaps of ashes. He made them an example of what will happen to ungodly people. But God also rescued Lot out of Sodom because he was a righteous man who was sick of the shameful immorality of the wicked people around him" (2 Peter 2:4-7, NLT). That was stern, isn't it? We need that knowledge.

We should not allow those dealings of God with men in the past go down as mere bed-time stories. They were written for us to learn and take heed. Eli the High Priest and his children became victims of a devastating judgment of God when they refused to hear and heed His warnings. The Lord sent His warnings to Eli through Samuel, saying. "Behold, I will do something in Israel at which both ears of everyone who hears it will tingle. In that day I will perform against Eli all that

I have spoken concerning his house, from beginning to end. For I have told him that I will judge his house forever for the iniquity which he knows, because his sons made themselves vile, and he did not restrain them. And therefore I have sworn to the house of Eli that the iniquity of Eli's house shall not be atoned for by sacrifice or offering forever" (1 Sam 3:11-14, NKJV). Why is the judgment coming? God warned Eli, but he did not restrain the children. When Samuel told Eli what the Lord told him, Eli said, "He is the Lord, let Him do what seems good to Him".

Men and brethren, it is only a tree that will be told, "I will cut you down tomorrow", and you will come back tomorrow, and still find that tree standing. We are human beings, for crying out loud; created with conscience and common sense. May God grant us the grace to seek to know Him intimately enough to know that He does not play around with words. The family of Eli was destroyed in a most dramatic way when he chose to do nothing to avert this judgment. The children of Israel went out to war against the Philistines; Israel lost four thousand soldiers. Rather than seek God's face to know why they failed, they went and brought the Ark of God to the battle ground; something that has never happened before. The soldiers of Israel were killed again; thirty thousand soldiers this time. When the news came to Eli that Israel has been defeated by the Philistines, and that his people have been slaughtered, his two sons, Hophni and Phinehas, were also killed. And the Ark of God has been captured (1 Sam.4:17, NLT); Eli slumped and gave up. Israel, lost her glory in one swoop, and became Ichabod. What an avoidable tragedy!

God our Father does not delight in watching His children groan under His judgment, but we leave Him with no choice when we choose to reject His counsel and pay no attention to His corrections. In a prophetic song, God lamented over His relationship with Israel and how they had continued to frustrate His loving kindness over them.

"Now I will sing for the one I love; a song about his vineyard: My beloved had a vineyard, on a rich and fertile hill. He plowed the land, cleared its stones, and planted it with the best vines. In the middle he built a watchtower and carved a winepress in the nearby rocks. Then he waited for a harvest of sweet grapes, but the grapes that grew were bitter" (Isa. 5:1,2, NLT). What a passionate cry of disappointment? Are you not touched by this heart cry?

Now, who planted this vineyard? Who does this vineyard represent? "The vineyard of the Lord of hosts is the house of Israel, and the men of Judah are His pleasant plant. He looked for justice, but behold, oppression; for righteousness, but behold, a cry for help" (Isa.5:7, NKJV). This is a representation of the way the present day Church, today's Israel, have been treating God. All we do daily is cry to God to fill our insatiable desires, even while living in disobedience. God keeps asking us daily, "Is it not natural to expect good fruits after investing so much in the lives of mankind?" Having given the world His only begotten Son to die for us, God the Father pleads with our good sense of judgment: "What more could have been done to My vineyard that I have not done in it? Why then, when I expected it to bring forth good grapes, did it bring forth wild grapes?" (Isa.5:4, NKJV).

At this point, men leave God with no choice but to execute judgment upon an evil and disobedient generation. Hence the Lord followed up this heart cry with judgment which becomes inevitable at this point. "Now, please let Me tell you what I will do to My vineyard: I will take away its hedge, and it shall be burned; And break down its wall, and it shall be trampled down. I will lay it waste; it shall not be pruned or dug, but there shall come up briers and thorns. I will also command the clouds that they rain no rain on it" (Isa 5:5-6, NKJV). Hmmm, dearly beloved, we should pray never to become so careless to a point of not being sensitive to God's warnings.

So many Christians are already suffering under some form of divine judgment or another. When we humble ourselves and return to God in repentance, we save ourselves from His eternal judgment. But when we remain proud and stubborn, Paul, the Apostle said, "if we deliberately keep on sinning after receiving the knowledge of the truth, no further sacrifice for sins is left for us, but only a certain fearful expectation of judgment and a fury of fire that will consume God's enemies" (Heb 10:26-27, NLT). Can you stand that? Giving ourselves to knowing God's judgment, will save us from continuing in any matter of defiance of

God's warnings. The worst thing that can happen to a man in this world is not untimely death; not the death of a mother, father, wife, husband or a loved one; not even living a poverty-stricken life that makes you the mockery of the town. The worst thing that can happen to any living mortal under the sun is to die unprepared to face God's judgment.

There is only one way to escape unpleasant surprises on the Day of Judgment. God is a just God. If we give ourselves to understand the nature of His judgment, it will help us to judge ourselves daily in His presence in all sincerity. We cannot afford to sweep anything under the carpet, knowing that in His judgment, there is nothing hidden that shall not be made open. The only possible reason why a famous 'prophet or pastor miracle worker' would be told by the Lord, "Depart, I don't know you", must be because we took Him for granted. When we are busy prophesying and, doing all the miracles for the carnal glory of men, we tend to forget His judgment. Our saving grace comes only from a personal commitment to seek the intimate knowledge of God until the fear of His judgment grips us.

CONCLUSION

ONE serious matter that requires our attention here as we bring this revelation to conclusion is this: do you know that if you miss heaven, you will never escape the lake of fire? If the Lord tells you, "Depart, I don't know you", the Satan that deceived you, and governs the pit of hell will be handy to take the victim to the bottomless pit. Again, worthy of note is the fact that there is no hint in the Bible of any possibility to transfer from lake of fire to Heaven while eternity lasts. Remember what Father Abraham told the rich man who pleaded from hell that Lazarus should come from Abraham's bosom to cool his thirst with a drop of water; Abraham said, "… between us and you there is a great gulf fixed: so that they which would pass from hence to you cannot; neither can they pass to us, that would come from thence (Luke 16:26). If we truly believe this Bible, there is no way we should allow ourselves to go through this life unprepared to meet with the Lord.

Recommended Books For Studying When sitting In God's Presence

1) Knowing God Personally Vol.1 (The Intimate Dimension) By Godson Hez
2) Knowing God Personally Vol. 2 (Seeking Divine Perspective) By Godson Hez
3) Fresh Fire For Fresh Result By Godson Hez
4) We Need Revival, Not Survival By Godson Hez
5) Tortured For Christ By Richard Wurmbrand
6) Whose Image Are You By Lafamcall Ministries
7) Becoming Like Jesus By Gbinle Akanni
8) The Journey To The Wealthy Place By Ngozi Favour Anyaora
9) The Final Quest By Rick joyner
10) The Call By Rick Joyner
11) The Sword By Rick Joyner
12) The Path By Rick Joyner
13) I Dare To Call Him, Father By Bilquish Sheikh
14) And other Revival Books

www.ingramcontent.com/pod-product-compliance
Lightning Source LLC
Chambersburg PA
CBHW070054120526
44588CB00033B/1428